Heart of Ice:
Tracking the Wendigo

Jason Hewlett

Heart of Ice:
Tracking the Wendigo

This edition published by Small Town Monsters
Publishing, LLC in 2025

Author: Jason Hewlett
Cover Artist: Jeff Kunze

Table of Contents

Foreword

The wendigo, a chilling specter of Algonquian lore, is more than a mere myth – it is a haunting presence deeply woven into the cultural and legal history of Canada, particularly in the frigid wilderness of Alberta.

This malevolent entity, described as a cannibalistic spirit or monstrous being, thrives in tales of isolation, starvation, and greed, embodying the harsh realities of survival in the northern boreal forests. Its legend endures not only as folklore but also as a stark reminder of humanity's fragility when confronted with nature's merciless indifference.

Being from Alberta myself, I am aware of the aggressiveness of the prairie winter. As I type this, the temperatures are plunging to -40 C tonight as it often does in January months. One can only imagine, as I am cooped up in my warm house, what this would mean for First Nations people and settlers who had no such luxuries. Being unable to get out of such deadly cold, where your skin is likely to freeze off in under five minutes, would look much different at a time where man-made heat sources were not available.

In the icy reaches of Alberta – Slave Lake, Lesser Slave Lake, and Fort Saskatchewan – the wendigo's shadow looms large. Historical accounts intertwine with Indigenous oral traditions to paint a vivid picture of this creature's terrifying influence. The wendigo is said to emerge when extreme cold and hunger drive individuals to acts of desperation, such as cannibalism. This transformation into a wendigo is not merely physical but spiritual – a corruption of the soul that turns humans into insatiable monsters. According to Cree and Algonquian beliefs, the wendigo is both a cautionary tale and an embodiment of winter's cruelty.

The legend gained notoriety in Alberta's legal history during the late nineteenth century. Cases like that of Swift Runner in 1879 shocked settlers and Indigenous communities alike. A Cree hunter, Swift Runner claimed he was possessed by a wendigo spirit when he killed and consumed his family during a brutal winter. His trial and subsequent execution highlighted the collision between Indigenous spiritual explanations and Canadian law. Similarly, other cases in Northern Alberta reveal how fear of the wendigo influenced both Indigenous justice practices and colonial legal systems.

The wendigo's characteristics: its gaunt frame, icy heart, and insatiable hunger mirror the desolation of Alberta's frozen wilderness. It is said to stalk its victims silently through snow-covered forests, its approach heralded by an unnatural chill or foul stench. Some believe it can mimic human voices to lure prey into the woods, where it consumes not just flesh but also humanity itself. The creature's greed serves as a moral lesson against selfishness and isolation, values essential for survival in harsh climates. But is it just a folktale – a warning like the potential of getting coal in your stocking at Christmas?

Even today, whispers of the wendigo persist. Locals recount eerie sightings near Slave Lake or strange occurrences in Fort Saskatchewan's dense forests. These stories suggest that the wendigo is not merely a relic of the past but a living presence – a reminder that some mysteries defy explanation. Whether as metaphor or real entity, the wendigo continues to hold sway over imaginations, blending history, myth, and fear into an enduring legend etched into Alberta's frozen landscape.

The psychological implications of the wendigo in modern psychiatric practices are deeply tied to its cultural and symbolic significance, particularly through the lens of "Wendigo Psychosis," a controversial culture-bound syndrome. This condition is characterized by paranoia, anxiety, hallucinations, and cannibalistic urges, often emerging in individuals under extreme stress, isolation, or starvation. It is thought to arise from a fusion of cultural narratives and psychological vulnerabilities, offering an outlet for internal distress.

Oddly, however, there are some issues with this as a blanket diagnosis. One example is the Swift Runner case in Alberta, where starvation was reportedly not a factor in the decision to kill and eat his family. It also fails to explain why certain "cures" did in fact seem to work with no recurrence of the psychosis, such as drinking hot tallow. As we well know, such a simple cure does nothing to alleviate a deep psychosis breakdown in any other known mental disorders. If it does provide temporary relief, then there is a repeat of symptoms later. We do not see that in certain documented cases of Wendigo Psychosis, which, once again, puts the questionable diagnosis on the table for debate.

From a psychological perspective, Wendigo Psychosis reflects mechanisms like externalization and self-fulfilling prophecy. Externalization allows individuals to project their cannibalistic thoughts onto a potential mythical wendigo, creating a psychological buffer to cope with guilt and social stigma. Similarly, the self-fulfilling prophecy theory suggests that deep-seated fears of becoming a wendigo can lead individuals to unconsciously adopt behaviors that align with this belief. These frameworks highlight how cultural myths shape mental health experiences.

Understanding Wendigo Psychosis also emphasizes the importance of cultural sensitivity in psychiatric care. By respecting Indigenous beliefs about the wendigo, mental health professionals can better address psychotic symptoms within their cultural context. This approach fosters empathy and helps develop coping strategies that resonate with patients' values and experiences. Does it explain all cases? No. Which leaves us wondering as a society: what exactly is going on here? What does it mean if there is truth to the wendigo lore?

The wendigo is terrifying for reasons that transcend its grotesque appearance and cannibalistic hunger – it embodies the darkest fears of humanity, rooted in survival, morality, and the fragility of civilization. If this creature is real, it would shatter the boundaries between myth and reality, forcing us to confront not only its horrifying existence, but also what it reveals about our own nature.

The wendigo legend originates from Algonquian-speaking Indigenous peoples of North America, particularly in regions like Canada's boreal forests. It is described as a gaunt, skeletal being with sunken eyes, decaying flesh, and a heart of ice. Its most chilling feature is its insatiable hunger for human flesh- a craving that can never be satisfied. This endless hunger is not just physical but symbolic. It reflects greed, selfishness, and the loss of humanity. The wendigo's grotesque form mirrors the consequences of succumbing to these impulses: a monstrous transformation that leaves the individual cursed to wander the wilderness eternally in search of victims.

What makes the wendigo particularly terrifying is its connection to winter and famine. In Northern Canada's harsh winters, starvation was historically a very real threat. The wendigo myth emerged as both a cautionary tale and a psychological coping mechanism for communities facing such dire conditions. It warned against cannibalism as the ultimate taboo – an act that could strip away one's humanity and invite possession by this malevolent spirit. The wendigo's ability to mimic human voices adds another layer of horror, luring victims into its grasp with false hope before consuming them.

If the wendigo were real, it would mean that this creature is not merely a metaphor but an actual predator stalking the frozen wilderness. Reports of supposed encounters lend credence to this possibility. Eyewitnesses describe shadowy figures lurking in forests or hearing unearthly cries echoing through the night. Some claim to have experienced "Wendigo Fever," a mysterious affliction marked by foul odors, nightmares, and an uncontrollable urge to flee into the woods – never to be seen again. These accounts suggest that the wendigo operates on both physical and psychological levels, preying on fear and despair as much as on flesh.

The historical record also raises unsettling questions about the wendigo's reality. Cases like that of Swift Runner in 1879 were attributed to wendigo possession. Swift Runner himself claimed he was overtaken by the spirit of the wendigo, a belief shared by his community. Similarly, Jack Fiddler, an Indigenous shaman in Ontario, was known for "killing" individuals he believed were transforming into wendigos. These cases blur the line between myth and mental illness, suggesting that belief in the wendigo, or perhaps the wendigo itself, has tangible effects on human behavior.

Psychologically, the wendigo taps into universal fears: isolation, starvation, and moral collapse. Its legend serves as a warning about what happens when survival instincts override communal values. In Indigenous cultures, sharing resources was essential for survival in harsh environments; greed or hoarding could mean death for others. The wendigo embodies this selfishness taken to its extreme – a creature driven by endless consumption at the expense of others. In modern times, it has become a metaphor for societal issues like capitalism and environmental destruction – forces that consume without regard for sustainability or humanity.

If we accept that the wendigo might be real, its implications are profound. First, it would challenge our understanding of nature and reality itself. Could such a creature exist undetected in Canada's vast wilderness? Its association with winter storms and extreme weather suggests it may have powers beyond our comprehension – perhaps even influencing natural phenomena. Second, it would force us to reconsider our own capacity for monstrosity. The transformation into a wendigo begins with human choices: greed, desperation, or cannibalism. If such transformations are possible, what does that say about humanity's potential for darkness?

Moreover, belief in the wendigo has already shaped legal and cultural practices in Canada. Historical cases show how Indigenous communities used the legend to enforce moral behavior and address taboo subjects like cannibalism. Even today, stories of the wendigo persist in popular culture and local folklore, keeping its legacy alive as both a supernatural entity and a cautionary tale. If these stories are more than mere fiction – if they are rooted in actual encounters – it would validate centuries of Indigenous knowledge while raising new fears about what else might lurk in the shadows.

I have had strange encounters in the Alberta wilderness as have people I've interviewed over my twenty-three-year career in parapsychology. One of the most noted was a woman who had gone hunting with her friends in Edson, Alberta, in an area off the beaten path from the normal game trails. They had not been out long before they heard what sounded like a deer or elk making disturbing noises. She reported to me that they couldn't see anything but noted the noise was coming from a stand of trees ahead of them. She said the noise sounded almost mechanical, as if it was something's best attempt at sounding like a deer or elk. Now this is a woman who has grown up in the wilds of Alberta and is well versed in wildlife and taxidermy, and she said her blood ran cold at the sound. She told me that she felt an increasing level of threat she had not felt before in any woods. When the group of friends did not approach this sound, a voice then came out of the same spot where the deer noise was previously. She said it sounded like a poor imitation of a female voice begging for help. The woman told me that not one person with her was settled with the idea that this was a genuine human being. There were no footsteps around them as if someone had been there before, they could see no sign of life in the direction of the voice, and the voice itself felt to them like a deceptive lure. Their instinct would normally be to run for help, and in this case, everything in her being told her to get out immediately. The group made it back to the road to safety, but she felt as if she had narrowly escaped the grip of something terrifying. No one said a word on the way back to the town, and none of them spoke of it again.

I have had similar experiences in the woods of Alberta, including a moment where the sound of a friend's dog was mimicked as if it were in pain. When we checked on the dog, it was in the house, not the woods, and was just fine. At another time, a group of researchers and I had been out in Southern Alberta and saw a strange, gaunt, rail-thin figure disappear into a light formation in the dark, never to be seen again. Four intelligent, insightful and aware witnesses, and none of us could explain what we had just seen. The figure caused us no problems but stared at us for several seconds before turning around and disappearing right before our eyes.

Are these two examples proof of wendigo? No, but it absolutely reshaped our views on what reality looks like without the tainted spin with which we often blur it. *Something* is there. The woods have always held within us a deep-seated fear and often we chalk that up to a natural fear of predators and the unknown…but is it that simple? Is that what's going on here? Or are we inherently perceiving something far greater with our sixth sense than we would like to believe?

It's a chilling thought to entertain the notion that what we always considered the 'boogeyman under the bed' has its roots in truth, but the reality is that most folklore does. In western culture, we tend to brush aside Indigenous tales thinking they are simply nonsense of a bygone age, but that's simply an ignorant position to take. Are we doing it because we truly think it's just folktales, or are we doing it because we are afraid what it will mean for us if the wendigo turns out to be something more? One thing I have learned about guerilla skeptics over the years is that often, when presented with strong evidence, confirmation bias kicks in and they deny it all. Fear can be a funny thing.

Ultimately, what makes the wendigo so terrifying is not just its monstrous form or predatory nature but what it represents: the fragility of human morality under extreme conditions. It forces us to confront uncomfortable truths about survival and greed while reminding us of our vulnerability in an indifferent world. Whether real or metaphorical, the wendigo remains one of folklore's most haunting creations – a creature born from winter's cruel embrace yet capable of exposing humanity's deepest fears.

Now, if you're ready, let Jason Hewlett walk you down this rabbit hole of wendigo lore and see if you can stroll the winter trails again without peering over your shoulder at least once. Pack your tallow, make sure the fire is hot, and keep your axe close. This is one wild ride.

–*Morgan Knudsen*

Why Write a Book About the Wendigo?

Like a lot of children from my generation, I read comic books when I was a kid. One of the titles I read with regularity was The Incredible Hulk.

I don't remember what year it was or my age at the time, but I'd picked up an issue of The Incredible Hulk from a second-hand shop, largely because it featured a large, white, hairy monster trading blows with the not-so jolly green giant. Text on the cover read "In the wilds of Canada, ol' green skin takes on the weird, way-out wendigo – the thing that walks like a man!"

Come on! Who wouldn't want to read that?

The issue was The Incredible Hulk No. 162. It came out in April of 1973, although I read it several years later. The creature appeared in several Hulk stories in the ensuing years where it would not only go toe-to-toe with ol' green skin, but the ever-popular Wolverine and even a comic-book version of Sasquatch.

The character was so cool I ended up drawing my own interpretations in comics I was creating at the time. I thought the wendigo, or, as it was sometimes referred in the hollowed pages of Marvel Comics, the Wen-Di-Go, was one of the best bad guys I'd ever seen. The fact he could punch it out with the likes of the Hulk made him even better.

What I didn't realize at the time was the wendigo wasn't a comic-book villain created by Marvel Comics writers Steve Englehart and Herb Trimpe. The wendigo featured in Marvel Comics is an Indigenous legend that, in the four-color world of comics books, was attributed strictly to the Algonquian peoples of Eastern Canada.

As I grew older and studied the story more seriously, I learned Engelhart and Trimpe got a lot correct about the wendigo, at least in terms of what they needed for a comic-book villain. The wendigo isn't a specific person but is instead the manifestation of a curse that strikes anyone who commits an act of cannibalism in the Canadian North Woods. However, as I grew older, I learned the wendigo legend isn't quite that simple.

But I'm getting ahead of myself.

As the years went by and my interest in the paranormal grew, I realized the wendigo wasn't a made-up character, but a very real Indigenous folk story that carried as much weight for believers as other First Nations legends like Bigfoot and Ogopogo, which are prominent in my home province of British Columbia in Western Canada. In time I realized one thing Englehart and Trimpe failed to mention is the wendigo isn't exclusive to Eastern Canada, as from time to time I heard reports out of Alberta, a neighboring province east of mine. As the years passed, I learned the legend itself was born in Northern Alberta, about a twelve-hour drive from where I live.

My interest in the paranormal began because of a terrifying incident I had when I was five. I was sitting in the back of my mom's hatchback, which was parked outside a friend's house. The friend was going to stay at our place for a sleepover, and my mom had gone to fetch him. I waited in the car and was staring at the empty street in front of me when a face appeared in the window. One second it wasn't there, then it was. It was a monstrous face with twisted features (not unlike an unmasked Jason Voorhees, for those of you familiar with this horror movie icon). As quickly as it appeared, it then disappeared, and I was left cowering on the floor of the car in fear. Neither my friend nor my mom had seen what happened and both confirmed no one was on the street at the time, let alone lurking around the car.

The experience opened my mind to the idea of ghosts and other supernatural beings and, as I grew up, I took a more serious interest in researching various high strangeness. I went on my first paranormal investigation more than twenty years ago and eventually formed the Canadian Paranormal Society along with my friend, mentor and fellow investigator Peter Renn.

Most of our work, and my interest in the paranormal, has focused on ghosts and hauntings and related phenomena. I've never fancied myself a cryptozoologist – someone who tries to find, describe or study creatures that appear in stories and which some people believe exist or say they've seen – or a monster hunter. It's not that the subject doesn't interest me, but it's not something I put much energy into.

Then the COVID-19 pandemic happened, and it became increasingly difficult to gain access to places believed to house ghosts. Renn and I had created a web series called *We*

Want to Believe, which documented our investigations, and it ran on a YouTube channel called *The Paranormal Network*. We needed content and thought the best way to keep the show going was to go on a hunt for Bigfoot, which meant we could investigate, film outside, and remain socially distanced while doing it. The efforts proved successful and my interest in hunting monsters was born.

A few years later I joined friend, filmmaker, and fellow cryptid enthusiast Eli Watson on an expedition to Okanagan Lake in search of the lake monster known as Ogopogo. Our efforts are well documented in the documentary *Cursed Waters: Creature of Lake Okanagan* and the accompanying book I wrote, *The Legend of Ogopogo: Canada's Loch Ness Monster*, both of which are available from Small Town Monsters.

What's all this have to do with the wendigo, you ask? Patience, I'm getting to that.

The experience I had researching Ogopogo and working on *Cursed Waters*, not to mention the Bigfoot hunts on which my Canadian Paranormal Society colleagues and I embarked, further whetted my appetite for monsters. Once the dust had settled from Ogopogo, I found myself wanting to take another deep dive into a cryptid-related topic. I was scrolling through the Internet one day, digging into the Cadborosaurus legend, which relates to a sea monster off the coast of British Columbia, and the story of the wendigo, which intrigued me. Although I love sea and lake monsters, I was drawn deep into the dark heart of the wendigo folktale.

The wendigo is far more frightening than anything depicted in the comic books I read as a boy. People are still seeing it to this day in rural Alberta and even in the suburbs of Vancouver, British Columbia. In fact, the story is so frightening to some that even mentioning the creature's name has people afraid they will summon the spirit – an act which could open them to possession, turning them into a cold-heart cannibal.

Knowing that, how could one not want to learn even more?

So, come with me as I unravel not only the wendigo's origins, but also embark on my own quest to track down the legendary creature for myself. As you will soon find, this effort is not for the faint of heart – and the story is as frightening as any modern horror film.

Fact from Fiction

How is this for a scary story to kick things off?

The hamlet of Fort Kent is in Northern Alberta near the border of Saskatchewan, the next most eastern province in Canada. It is small, with a population of some two hundred and fifty-four people as of 2021. It is often considered a remote hunting and fishing destination for enthusiasts.

Northern Alberta is barren and flat, with stands of trees and forest scattered about. One can stand atop one of the many rolling hills and see for miles. In the winter it becomes so cold and snowy that it is nearly inhospitable.

And – if you believe the legend – it is the location of a brutal massacre attributed to the wendigo.

As the story goes, Fort Kent had begun to dwindle in size from the vibrant logging community it was in the early 1900s to the hamlet it would become when, in the 1920s, a mysterious predator took up residence in the nearby woods. Ranchers would venture to their stables to feed their horses in the morning only to find the animals mutilated. Their cattle were found disemboweled in their fields. Once the sun set, otherworldly howls came from the woods behind their homes.

If you believe the story, one resident ventured into the night armed with shotgun intent on killing whatever it was that preyed on their livestock. He reported seeing a dark shadow with bright glowing eyes darting between the trees.

According to the *Lakeland Connect*, a news and entertainment media company in Bonnyville, about a fifteen-minute drive from Fort Kent, a young English doctor named Thomas Burton arrived in Fort Kent shortly after these animal attacks began. Burton had been a combat surgeon during World War One, and his senses were reeling from the carnage he had witnessed. He hoped the move to Fort Kent would help him leave behind these horrible memories.

Burton's first task was to treat an outbreak of smallpox in the hamlet, which he initially succeeded in doing. The townsfolk embraced him and his wife, Katie. Unfortunately, the disease's spread suddenly became uncontrollable, and Burton was overwhelmed with the sick and dying.

Sadly, it didn't take long for Katie to fall ill, and, when she succumbed to the sickness, Burton is said to have locked himself away with her dead body. As the days ticked by, Burton went mad with grief and was possessed by the wendigo. Under its influence, he ate his wife's flesh. When done with her, he allegedly went on a killing spree for the next three days.

Few were spared during this massacre. By the end of the third day, only eleven of Fort Kent's one hundred and fifty residents remained.

"He went out, door-to-door, in Fort Kent, and killed the people who lived in Fort Kent," said Jenna Colbourne, the owner of *Lakeland Connect*.

"It was a big massacre; so much so that they actually picked up and moved the town across where the street is now."

While visiting Fort Kent today, one can easily see where the original town was and the new town begins, said Colbourne. The dividing line between the original settlement and the current one is now a highway.

According to the accounts Colbourne has read, the massacre was not discovered right away. It was only when the postman arrived to deliver his weekly load of mail that all the bodies were found.

A separate account reads that one resident who had managed to avoid the smallpox contagion left Fort Kent to seek help from a nearby settlement. Several days later he and a handful of volunteers rode into Fort Kent with supplies. They found the town cloaked in an eerie silence broken only by the buzzing of flies and smell of blood.

In this version of the tale, there were twenty-four victims, most found dead in their beds, having been slaughtered in their sleep. Some of the bodies were partially eaten.

The only townsperson unaccounted for in any version of the legend is Thomas Burton. Officers with the North-West Mountain Police investigated, and suspected Burton had finally lost his mind and gone on the killing spree. His work done, he wandered off into the woods.

Members of the local Cree tribe believe Burton had been possessed by the wendigo, an evil cannibalistic spirit that haunted the northern wilderness.

The story is well known in the area, to the point that it has become the stuff of urban legend. If one were to approach a Bonnyville or Fort Kent resident today and mention the wendigo, Colbourne says they will know exactly what you are talking about.

"And if they don't, they will have just moved to town," she said.

Colbourne grew up in a town called Elk Point, which is about a forty five-minute drive from Fort Kent, and she never heard of the story until moving to the Fort Kent area, she said.

"What I did hear as a kid is that if you laughed at the northern lights, you would go crazy and you'd become demonic and kill people," said Colbourne. "So, I've always wondered if there was a tie between the two because of the Indigenous element."

The thing is the story of the Fort Kent massacre is just that – a story. Researcher Morgan Knudsen of the *Supernatural Circumstances* podcast said the Fort Kent massacre was concocted by a writer for a movie called *The Lost Town of Fort Kent: The Fort Kent Wendigo*. The film went into pre-production in the early 2000s but was never finished. The story, however, was circulated around the Internet.

"A show called *Creepy Canada* picked it up as fact and it just snowballed," she said.

Indeed, I was fooled by the Fort Kent story, having encountered it during my early days of research for this book. In addition to the *Lakeland Connect*, the urban legend appeared on the *Mysteries of Canada* website, on an episode of *The Midnight Train* podcast, various Reddit threads, and, naturally, *The Lost Town of Fort Kent: The Fort Kent Wendigo* page on Facebook, which was a promotional tool for the unmade film. It was only an article on *werewolves.com* that pointed out the legend to be a work of fiction.

Why invent a story about the wendigo when the real story is just as, if not more so, terrifying than anything someone could concoct? I will be diving deeper into the legend of the wendigo in the ensuing pages. However, I believe it is vital to first understand the effect stories like this have on us as a society and how they can be spun out of control by popular culture.

To address this, I turned to my friend and fellow paranormal enthusiast Mr. Sam Shearon. Shearon is a British born dark artist who specializes in horror and science-fiction, drawing from his love of monsters, madmen, dark futures and the work of H.P. Lovecraft and Clive Barker. In fact, he has provided illustrations for those very volumes as well as crafted covers for such comic books as *Judge Dredd*, *The X-Files* and *Mars Attacks*. He has also created sleeve artwork for the rock bands Ministry, Rob Zombie, and Iron Maiden, to name just a few.

Shearon happens to also be a wealth of knowledge on all things in the high strangeness realm, which is why I knew that I had to ask him about the appeal of the wendigo.

"I think part of it is the name. It's the same with the word Sasquatch. It's such an exotic name if you think outside of the English language. *Wendigo*. That's such a strange name but it also has that echo of Native America, which is mystical and fascinating."

Even though Western culture has lived side-by-side with Indigenous people for hundreds of years, the average person knows little to nothing about Native American beliefs and religions, he emphasized. So, when someone hears the term

10

wendigo it automatically sparks images of something exotic, strange, and frightening.

Because few people have taken the time to research Indigenous beliefs and folklore, pop culture becomes the frame of reference for stories like the wendigo. In addition to appearing in comics, the wendigo has also turned up in a variety of motion pictures, including the 2021 release *Antlers* from *Crazy Heart* director Scott Cooper.

If you have not yet watched it, *Antlers* is worth your time. It takes a serious approach to the material by considering the connection between the wendigo topic to its Algonquin legend roots. The creature design is also very good, although it sticks with the popular representation of the wendigo having deer-like antlers. This is an aspect which is not exactly true, according to legend.

Shearon said the wendigo was never attributed to being an actual physical creature until Algernon Blackwood's 1910 novella, appropriately titled *The Wendigo*. Prior to that book, wendigo was terminology for a person's behavior. Blackwood's story turned it into a mythical creature. It should be noted that, in this initial representation, the antlers were not present.

Many Pagan, Indigenous, and non-Christian religions depict various beings as having antlers or horns. In addition, Native Americans will, at times, wear headdresses and outfits adorned with similar visual representation as part of certain ceremonies. As early Christians took over Europe, other countries, and continents, they demonized the locally worshipped gods by saying those entities resembled the Christian Devil. This was one method of conversion – turning their local deities into something evil.

"Anything that's wrong or evil or is the Boogeyman in general will have horns," said Shearon.

As the wendigo story progressed through time, the image of the stag's head with antlers became associated with it, as did the notion of it being an actual creature instead of a frame of mind or behavior.

"Which is strange because we know stags are vegetarian. Of all the things that will get you and eat you, a stag's not one of them."

It is the weird, spooky nature of the wendigo that makes it so accessible, emphasized Shearon. Much like a Bigfoot, Ogopogo, or a Tim Burton film, it is something that becomes fun and somewhat easy to embrace because of how different and strange it is.

"You can bring it into your own living room and have models and plushies and toys of it. It becomes something you want to explore and that's why, for decades, it's continued in popularity. Much like Sasquatch."

Antlers does a good job of mixing all aspects of the wendigo story into one narrative, Shearon said. Other wendigo-themed movies include *Dark Was the Night*, *Devil in the Dark*, *The Retreat*, the appropriately titled *The Wendigo*, and *Dawn of the Beast* – which also includes Bigfoot. Although it does not directly mention the wendigo or show any monsters, the 1999 Guy Pearce movie *Ravenous* does deal with cannibalism as a form of possession.

These films take the wendigo story with varying degrees of seriousness. Viewers should be aware that some of these movies play a bit recklessly with the actual legend. This, of course, is nothing new in Hollywood. As I mentioned in my previous books, just because something is based on a true story, does not equate to the finished product being entirely factual. Much like the Fort Kent Massacre, the initial concept often has elements of truth while the ensuing details are often overhyped, if not downright entirely fictionalized.

I like to pick on *The Conjuring 2* as a prime example. The sequel finds real-life paranormal investigators Ed and Lorraine Warren investigating the Enfield Poltergeist, a very real haunting that occurred in England between 1977 and 1979. It was well documented by Maurice Grosse and Guy Lyon Playfair of the Society for Psychical Research.

The Warrens are front and center in the film and heavily involved in the investigation which, according to the movie, culminated in a showdown with a demon that was intent on killing Ed Warren. In truth, the Warrens had literally nothing to do with the Enfield investigation. In fact, when they approached the Society for Psychical Research, they were told to stay well away. Yet, because a movie was made about the case with them involved, and it was touted as being based on a true story, many people believe they were there.

Unfortunately, most people do not necessarily concern themselves with – or care about – the facts. By playing fast and loose with the truth one can take these scary stories, make them popular, and, in some cases, profit from them, asserted Shearon. People fear what they do not understand and do not know. If you can market that rather than explain it, you are bound to get more attention.

"Especially if you're the guy who knows all about it. You're the cool guy in town. All of a sudden, you're the ticket master," he said.

In a way this has happened in the world of cryptozoology. Cryptozoology is a pseudoscience and subculture that searches for and studies unknown, legendary, or extinct animals whose current existence is disputed or unsubstantiated. This includes lake monsters like the Loch Ness Monster and Ogopogo and wild men like Bigfoot.

However, Shearon points out a current trend where beings like Dogman, Mothman, the chupacabra and, yes, the wendigo – creatures more of supernatural origin than any flesh-and-blood animal that has lived on Earth – are now being lumped in with all the rest. As a result, they have become pop culture mainstays even though there is no actual proof that any of them exist, or have ever existed, outside of the realm of folk stories.

"On a natural history basis, there's no such creature. It makes no sense, yet it's become this popular trope that people buy into, sway their beliefs, and go 'Oh yeah, yeah. Maybe.'"

The wendigo is not just a folk story; it is an Indigenous legend. There is no way of avoiding that there is a long history of Western culture taking other culture's stories and adopting them as our own. I wrote a whole book about that very thing with *The Legend of Ogopogo: Canada's Loch Ness Monster*. Ogopogo is a made-up word for a monster alongside which the Westbank First Nations have lived for thousands of years. They call it N'ha-a-itk, and it is their water spirit. A dimension walker. The word Ogopogo was made up in a song that was somehow associated with what European settlers were seeing in Okanagan Lake and has since become a tourism mascot for the region.

What does the wendigo mean for Indigenous people? How do they feel about what the legend has become in popular culture? I turned to paranormal investigator Amanda Quill and Kenzie Taylor of the *Historical Natives* podcast for answers. Both are Indigenous and well versed in the wendigo.

Although Indigenous, Taylor was introduced to the wendigo through various media, including horror movies and television. She pointed out an episode of the popular TV show *Supernatural* featured the creature. From there, she backtracked and learned the story is a big part of the Algonquin-speaking people.

"And that's, like, a big umbrella of people," she said. This accounts for how widespread the wendigo story is known geographically.

Taylor believes the wendigo is less a folk story of legend and more a fable, or series of fables, that act as cautionary tales among Algonquin-speaking people.

"It's a story to tell children and to spook people to stop them from doing things that are thought to be taboo," said Taylor.

This fits with the research I have done and will share more of later. Every wendigo story or encounter starts with someone who has gone down a dark path by allowing greed or some other negative emotion to control them.

There is also, of course, the cannibalism aspect. When someone feasts on human flesh, they allow the wendigo spirit into them. What does Taylor think of that? She points out there are also stories that combine the two triggers, for lack of a better word. The person gives into greed and gluttony and is slowly transformed into a soulless cannibal who consumes their fellow man.

Those who become a wendigo do not die, she said. They can "starve out" from hunger but are doomed to wander the cold woods, possibly forever.

"I like to think they migrate with the temperatures because they do prefer the freezing temperature to normal [temperatures]," said Taylor.

Does this account for wendigo sightings that take place as far south as Missouri? It would make sense that wendigo would roam there during the winter months and move north when temperatures warmed. While the theory seems correct, Taylor asserts that people are mistaken about what they are seeing.

"Those are Skinwalkers." Taylor noted of the Missouri sightings.

"They are completely different entities entirely, and that's one thing that Western media – especially on TikTok – likes to get wrong."

In Navajo culture, a Skinwalker is a type of evil witch who can turn into, possess, or disguise themselves as an animal.

Quill is the founder of *Coldspotters*, a team of paranormal investigators who operate out of Vancouver, British Columbia, Canada. A member of the Cree tribe from the province of Manitoba, she grew up aware of the wendigo, or *wihtiko* as it is referred among the Cree people. She did not do a deep dive into the lore, however, until her team was called to the Vancouver suburb of Surrey to investigate a possible wendigo sighting.

We will discuss this case in detail later in the book. Quill, however, agrees with Taylor that the wendigo is very much a cautionary tale among her people – albeit one that is, at the same time, very real.

"These stories are coming from ancestors, and these stories are being told over all these years because there's a lesson there. There's something more that we need to be pulling from there," observed Quill.

When people succumb to things like greed, lust, or gluttony they lose something of themselves. Drug addiction, the criminal lifestyle, taking what you should not take, these are all things that make a person vulnerable to the wendigo spirit.

Quill does not mind how the wendigo story is told, be it in media or movies, as the cautionary nature of the wendigo needs to be heard to prevent people from falling prey to their baser emotions and, by default, the evil spirit waiting to take control of them.

We will discuss the wendigo as a cautionary tale further in a future chapter. However, before we delve any deeper into what the wendigo means and go in search of the creature itself in Northern Alberta, we need to return to an older time to reveal how the story eventually became established in modern culture.

We need to discuss the story of Swift Runner and other gruesome wendigo encounters from Canada's wild west.

How it All Began

Growing up in British Columbia, Canada, I was never privy to stories about the wendigo. As stated earlier, my first encounter was via a comic book and for years I thought the wendigo was a villain of the four-color world. When it came to monsters, the locals – Bigfoot and Ogopogo, the creature of Okanagan Lake – were my go-to.

However, people one province over grew up with stories about a different creature: one with a heart of ice that wandered the rolling prairie hills and scattered, dense forests of Northern Alberta. This creature was tall, with long limbs and a gaunt frame. It is called the wendigo. Simply mentioning its name can curse the speaker.

These stories are whispered quietly among residents, especially those living in rural communities where the tales are taken far more seriously. To a wider, more pop-culture-obsessed audience, however, the wendigo appears in children's books and as stuffed animals, especially at conventions about paranormal phenomena.

Morgan Knudsen grew up in Alberta and, like many children, has heard wendigo stories all her life. Although she is a parapsychology researcher, she never thought the creature to be real. Then she moved to Edmonton in the northern part of the province and learned that the creature's origin story touched on the town of Saint Albert, a smaller community a mere twenty minutes from her front door.

"Being a resident of Alberta, you quickly learn that this is something that's all over the place," she explained.

Like Bigfoot, Ogopogo, and Skinwalkers, the wendigo has been a part of Indigenous culture for hundreds, even thousands of years. Also, much like Bigfoot, the wendigo is described differently from tribe to tribe. Knudsen said some tribes describe a short creature with scraggily long hair and long claws while others report an inescapably tall being eight to twenty feet in height with a thin frame.

Some cultures believe the wendigo to be an external entity or creature. Others talk of it as being a person possessed by an evil spirit which forces evolution into a wendigo.

"Depending on where its life cycle sits, so to speak, its description can vary as well."

The one common denominator amongst all the iterations of the wendigo story is that this entity has a very skeletal frame with its internal organs often seen spilling from the body.

"Some cultures describe that the lips have been chewed off because this thing is so ravenously hungry, and that it's an entity born of famine, of depression, of isolation and that it roams oftentimes the wilderness, particularly in winter months, looking for food to satiate this ravenous hunger," she said.

A scholarly article written by Nathan D. Carlson of the University of Alberta, titled *Reviving Witiko (Wendigo): An Ethnohistory of "Cannibal Monsters" in the Athabasca*

District of Northern Alberta, 1878-1910, states the northern Alberta Cree and Metis sometimes describe the Witiko as an "owl-eyed monster with large clawed hands, matted hair, a naked emaciated body, and a heart made of solid ice."

"In essence, the Witiko's frightening and grotesque visage and its superhuman strength make it the consummate predator of humanity," writes Carlson.

He continues, stating the *witiko*, or wendigo, is also a term for an alleged mental condition believed to have affected Algonquians in northern remote areas. This "condition" is "an obsessive-compulsive anthropophagous inclination accompanied by homicidal behavior." Western culture describes this as Wendigo Psychosis, and it is something we will touch upon later in this book.

The wendigo was whispered about and feared in stories told long before any were written down. There is no one specific story that started it all. However, all such legends have a modern starting point – one specific tale that cements the creature into popular culture. For Bigfoot, it is the Patterson-Gimlin film. For Ogopogo, it is the John McDougal encounter on Okanagan Lake. For the wendigo, it is the story of Swift Runner.

Why Swift Runner? For one, he was the first person hanged by the North-West Mounted Police, an organization that would later become Canada's famous Royal Canadian Mounted Police, or RCMP, our national police force. His crimes were murder and acts of cannibalism. The execution occurred at Fort Saskatchewan on December 20, 1879, which newspaper and historical documents report as being a bitterly cold day.

According to an article published in *Old West* during the summer of 1990, Swift Runner was given the opportunity to address the crowd who gathered to watch his execution. He was unrepentant and "openly acknowledged his guilt and thanked his jailer for their kindness – then berated his guard for making him wait in the cold."

So, what happened with Swift Runner that resulted in him being sentenced to death?

Swift Runner was a Cree Indian who lived in central Alberta during the late 1800s. Up until the winter of 1878-1879 he lived quietly with this wife and children, traded with the Hudson's Bay Company, and served as a guide for the North-West Mounted Police, where he was well liked by the officers.

Depending on the version of the story, Swift Runner had either three children, five children, or six children. However, all versions of the story, including Swift Runner's own confession, report the winter of 1878-1879 was a time of starvation and misery for the Cree people and, because of these hardships, Swift Runner became possessed by a wendigo. He admittedly dismembered and consumed his wife and children.

"Some people say his mother-in-law and his brother were also eaten," explained Taylor. "But then, there are other things that I've researched that say it was his wife and children."

The events leading up to his possession are also well documented. Swift Runner had resided at Fort Kent but had become increasingly addicted to the same alcohol which he was employed to trade. He and his family were forced to leave the fort and Swift Runner decided to return to his Cree people. However, his behavior had become more violent due to his addiction. Swift Runner and his family were not welcome.

"He was exiled from them as well, so he was pushed into isolation with his family," continued Taylor, adding Swift Runner and his family moved to a cabin in the woods.

According to Carlson, this was in the Tawatinaw area near the Athabasca Landing trading post in north-central Alberta. Taylor said Swift Runner and his family were all seen alive in the fall of 1878. The following spring, only Swift Runner was left.

Knudsen emphasized that Swift Runner appeared at the Lacombe Mission in Saint Albert, where he was well known as a guide and trapper, one night in April of 1879. Banging on the mission's door to request access.

"He was saying that he was starving and that his family had passed away due to starvation over a horrible winter and they'd had no food."

What the parishioners, including Father Lacombe himself, saw did not make sense, however. At six-foot-four-inches and two hundred pounds, Swift Runner had always been an imposing figure. It was especially jarring that, despite his claims of starvation, he had not changed physically. Taylor adds to the tale, saying her research suggested he looked quite healthy.

"He looked rather plump," she explained.

"So, people in the town were like 'How did [his family] die of starvation and you look like that?' Something was just not adding up."

Knudsen added that Swift Runner displayed some odd behavior, especially after the sun set.

"And at nighttime they reported him screaming that this creature, a wendigo, which they had barely heard of at this point, was trying to get in the window to kill him."

Swift Runner spent several weeks at the Lacombe Mission under the watchful eyes of Father Lacombe and his parishioners. Knudsen explained that his behavior became increasingly strange, so when Swift Runner offered to take some of the children out for a hike, alarm bells went off in people's minds.

"Something is not right here. Where is this guy's family?" they wondered.

The North-West Mounted Police were notified, and constables arrived at the mission, demanding Swift Runner take them to the camp where he lived with his family. What followed was a wild goose chase of sorts where Swift Runner led them all over the area before finally taking them to his family's camp. It was then that they found the children and adults deceased in a scene that can best be described as a massacre.

"They found bones littered everywhere," said Knudsen.

"There were skulls cracked open. Bones with the marrow sucked out. They found human fat wiped on the trees and the tree trunks because they had been boiled down and eaten."

Taylor further explained there are several versions of how the bodies were discovered. In one variation, Swift Runner came forward and admitted he had killed and eaten his family, which led police to go in search of the bodies. The other iteration substantiates Knudsen's and other researcher's reports, noting that Swift Runner's odd behavior led authorities to perform a "wellness check" on the family. It was during that investigation when the massacre was discovered.

Some accounts suggest Swift Runner coerced one of his family members to aid in the massacre, Taylor alleged.

"He convinced one of his younger sons to help with the murder of one of his other children and I believe the mom." Once they were all dead, then he killed the younger one and ate him.

According to Knudsen's research, Swift Runner behaved in a very bizarre fashion when the bodies of his loved ones were discovered.

"He went out onto the frozen lake, and he began to howl like, what they described, was like a wendigo."

In his thesis, Carlson states he was able to locate Swift Runner's confession, which was recorded by Father Hyppolyte Leduc at the St. Albert Catholic Mission near Fort Edmonton in 1879. Swift Runner claimed a wendigo took possession of his soul and "in order to live longer far from people, and to put out the way the only witness to my crime, I seized my gun and killed the last of my children and ate him as I had done the others."

Swift Runner claimed he was able to hunt several ducks for food and was not in a position of desperation or starvation. He had eaten the others in his camp because he was possessed. He decided to murder and consume his last child to remove any witnesses to what he had done.

Swift Runner was arrested and taken to the North-West Mounted Police detachment at Fort Saskatchewan. None of the guards wanted to watch over this imposing man while he sat in his cell. This was especially true at night when he would scream that a wendigo was trying to crawl through the bars of his cell window. He claimed the creature was intent on killing him.

Despite this frightening behavior, Swift Runner got on well with the officers at Fort Saskatchewan during the duration of what turned out to be a very short trial. Taylor explained that Swift Runner used the wendigo possession as his defense for the crimes he had committed.

"In his culture they believe that a spirit called the wendigo can possess you, and it forced him to slowly eat his family. He became haunted by dreams, and it just bled into him slowly and one day he was like, 'I'm going to kill and eat my family.'"

Swift Runner was charged with murder and scheduled to be executed by hanging.

According to *Murderpedia*, the sentence created a problem for police as

Swift Runner and Guard, 1879

they had never executed anyone in this fashion before. Staff Sergeant Fred Bagley, a bugler with the Mounties, was put in charge of the hanging. Although there was some fumbling when the noose was placed around his neck – hence Swift Runner complaining about spending so much time in the cold – he was successfully hanged.

Swift Runner was buried somewhere near the fort. Knudsen asserts the exact location is not known to this day.

Due to his confession, Swift Runner's case is the most substantive record of the wendigo, or as Carlson calls it, *witiko* anthropophagy; anthropophagy being the custom and practice of eating human flesh and organs by another human being. But it is not the only case on record. In fact, the research I conducted on Swift Runner and the wendigo folktale prompted me to travel to north-central Alberta in May of 2024. There I was joined by Knudsen and her *Supernatural Circumstances* co-host Michael Browne on an expedition where I not only followed Swift Runner's trail from the Tawatinaw Valley to Fort Saskatchewan but also visited the sites of other alleged Wendigo massacres and sightings.

But I'm getting ahead of myself, as these adventures are described later in the book.

Before we can discuss that adventure, there are a few more documented encounters that helped cement the wendigo in modern monster lore which deserve to be shared. One of the most notorious cases is that of Jack Fiddler.

In all honesty, I first heard the name Jack Fiddler in the video game *Until Dawn*. In that game, Fiddler is a hermit who lives in the Blackwood Mountains and hunts and traps wendigos, which are among the villains stalking and killing the game's heroes. He is portrayed via motion capture by Larry Fessenden, a horror writer and director who penned the game and clearly pulled elements from wendigo lore.

Jack Fiddler was a Cree chief and shaman of the Sucker tribe among the Anishinaabe people in what is now northwestern Ontario. Born in the late 1830s or early 1840s, Fiddler's true name was *Zhauwuno-geezhigo-gaubow*, meaning He Who Stands in the Southern Sky. As a shaman, like his father before him, he became famous for his alleged ability to conjure animals and protect people from spells.

Also of importance, at least to his people, he was one of the few of his tribe who possessed the ability to defeat the wendigo. To them, it was a creature which prayed on the Sucker people during all-to-frequent bouts of famine and disease.

Kenton de Jong is a Canadian travel blogger and true-crime podcaster who has an appreciation for cryptids and high strangeness. It was while researching the wendigo that he came across the name Jack Fiddler and was compelled to learn more.

"This doesn't seem right," de Jong remarked of the original article that mentioned Fiddler. "It seemed rehashed or recycled from another article. I had a *newspapers.com* account and I thought 'I have the date. I have the name. Let's look up the guy.'"

He found an article about Fiddler in the *Victoria Daily Times* published in 1907 about two Indigenous men from the Sucker tribe who had been arrested for murder. This incident had occurred in September of 1906. One of those men was Jack Fiddler, the other his brother Joseph.

The episode of de Jong's podcast, *Unsolved Canadian Mysteries*, focuses on the wendigo and whether de Jong and his co-host believe it to be a real creature. But de Jong was so fascinated by the Fiddler story that he wrote a blog post about it on Kenton de Jong Travel called *The Last of the Wendigo Hunters*.

As a young man, *Zhauwuno-geezhigo-gaubow* was likely involved in the fur trade and would visit Hudson's Bay Company (HBC) fur trading forts. During these brief visits, he developed the ability to fiddle and is said to have built quality instruments. The HBC traders frequently gave English nicknames to the natives and designated whole clans by the name of the primary leader. As a result, *Zhauwuno-geezhigo-gaubow* and his brother, Pesequan, became Jack and Joseph Fiddler and the Sucker tribe often appear in public record as the Fiddler tribe.

During his life, Jack Fiddler claimed he defeated fourteen wendigos. Some of these beasts were sent against the Fiddler tribe by enemy shamans, while others were members of his own people who were overcome by the insatiable, incurable desire to eat human flesh. He was usually asked by family members to kill a very sick loved one before they turned into a wendigo. In some cases, the wendigo would ask to be euthanized before the transformation could be completed. Fiddler's own brother, Peter Flett, was killed after he turned into one of the creatures when the food ran out during a trading expedition.

The Fiddlers typically strangled their victims and burned the bodies. De Jong says the wendigo is believed to be a creature of ice and hate. He emphasizes that the bodies must be burned so that the frozen heart melts. This would then free the person's spirit, and the body would remain too disfigured to rise again.

In early 1907, two constables with the North-West Mounted Police heard of Fiddler's campaign against the wendigos from Norman Rae, an in-law of the Fiddlers. The police wanted to bring Canadian law to the north, so the

Mounties went to Deer Lake and arrested Jack and Joseph Fiddler for the murder of Mrs. Thomas Fiddler, Joseph's daughter-in-law. This occurred in September of 1906.

"They immediately confessed that they had killed this woman the previous year and they [the Mounties] take them into custody," says de Jong.

It soon became clear to the officers that the Fiddlers had killed several people over the years. De Jong writes that Fiddler admitted to a Methodist minister that he had taken responsibility for fourteen such deaths. However, some documents put the number at twenty-six or even more than thirty!

At the time of his arrest, Fiddler was in his seventies and was described as looking "very frail, very weak."

"He has a weak heart. He falls down a lot," explains de Jong.

"He was a very old man."

In Fiddler's mind, he wasn't killing people. He was killing wendigos. These were not acts of murder. However, once word of the deaths reached the Europeans who settled in Canada, and the Fiddler brothers went on trial for their crimes, sensational news headlines soon appeared.

"The headlines just screamed devil worship and all that kind of stuff," states de Jong.

"Obviously that's not what's happening here. It's a different type of religion and culture."

While the Indigenous people saw Fiddler as working to help his people and stave off an evil, murderous creature, Western culture and law clearly saw things differently. The result was, as de Jong writes in his article, "one of the strangest court cases to have ever happened in Canada began to unfold."

Jack Fiddler did not live to stand trial. He escaped captivity and was found dead. Joseph Fiddler did see his day in court though.

The witnesses called to testify against Joseph Fiddler were largely themselves Indigenous people. However, when the trial concluded, Canadian law won out over Native beliefs and Joseph Fiddler was found guilty of murder. He was relocated to Stony Mountain Penitentiary where, due to his age and ill health, he spent most of his time in the hospital and died from tuberculosis.

Based on his research, does de Jong believe the Wendigo is real? Initially he believed all paranormal phenomena – be they ghosts, Bigfoot, or any spooky thing in between – were invented stories to keep people awake at night. However, after reading about the wendigo and interviewing people who believe they have seen the creature, his opinions have begun to shift.

"As long as you believe something exists, it does exist. If you believe Ogopogo is real, it's already real. If you believe the town of Wilno, Ontario, is infested with vampires, it already has vampires. If you believe the wendigo is out there, it's already out there. You already have the fear of it, the traditions based around it, the community consciousness of it. That's enough to make it real. If it's real or not is based on your perceptions."

That being said, de Jong isn't convinced the wendigo is a flesh-and-blood creature. But he does put stock in the Wendigo Psychosis phenomenon, which we will discuss shortly. Why? Based on his research, other cultures do have cases of starvation leading to cannibalism, but none have stories of people turning into violent, ravenous creatures as a result.

"It's a specific, North American psychosis," he explains.

De Jong points out the Fiddler story is not unique either. During his research, he came across many stories of people killing wendigos to protect their tribe or free the person possessed by these creatures… or, at the very least, save their soul. In one bizarre case, a weasel was sent into a wendigo's backside so it could crawl inside the body and eat the frozen heart!

"It's an insane story but that's one of the ones I came across," states de Jong. "It's a frequent occurrence in history and in stories of people finding ways to kill these creatures, and Jack Fiddler and Joseph Fiddler and others were just doing this as well."

One more bit of backstory we must visit before continuing is that of Trout Lake in Northern Alberta. I was unable to visit Trout Lake during my expedition due to time restraints and the distance needed to travel to get there, but I still want to share the tale as it is a part of wendigo lore.

This tale is born out of the Roman Catholics finding themselves at odds with other religious communities that were popping up during Alberta's frontier days. Knudsen explains that these religions essentially competed for followers amongst the populace that was not Catholic.

"The Roman Catholics and the Anglicans were very much at odds here."

During the tirade, another figurehead showed up: an Indigenous man who became known as the Wendigo

Prophet. Why? He attempted to start a religious movement based on the wendigo phenomenon, explains Knudsen. He preached that this giant creature was coming to possesses everyone and the only way to be saved was to join his religion. His pitch proved quite effective.

"People were so terrified of this that they locked themselves in their homes to the point where there were people that starved to death in their home for fear of running into this thing as it so called roamed the countryside."

Another Indigenous man known as Napanin, or Felix Auger as settlers came to know him, was not swayed by this story. Instead, he and his wife and children decided to leave the area and visit Napanin's family in Trout Lake.

Carlson's paper picks up the story from here. The family began their journey on January 1, 1896. Napanin's wife, Catherine, was pregnant at the time and the belief was this fifty-mile trek through deep snow, muskeg, and forest was being made so Napanin's family could be present for the child's birth.

Napanin drove his family via dogsled, and the first night passed uneventfully, Carlson wrote. But on the second night Napanin, who was reported to be in good health, saw something in the woods that evidently drove him insane!

While eating supper around the fire, Napanin suddenly said to this wife "See, look at that! It's coming for me!"

He hid under his blanket and told Catherine that one of the children looked to him like "a spring moose" and that he "wanted to kill and eat it." Catherine stayed awake all night fearful her husband would do something terrible.

The next morning, she suggested Napanin venture ahead on his own while she drove the sled dogs. Carlson wrote that

Napanin consented for a while but stopped suddenly, saying something would not let him go on.

Napanin did eventually move on, and the family finally arrived at Trout Lake. By then, however, Napanin was in a state of mental disaster, says Knudsen.

"He was violent. He was screaming. He was swelling up and producing all the signs of what we've come to know as Wendigo Psychosis."

The citizens of Trout Lake isolated Napanin in a cabin and even tried tying him down so he wouldn't harm anyone. However, he was in such a state that he was able to break his restraints, much to the terror of his family. He also continued to rant that he wanted to eat the children.

During what moments of lucidity that he had, Napanin asked that he be killed for fear of the wendigo taking him over.

One morning Napanin's nephew went into the cabin to check on him. Napanin had once again broken free of his bonds and attacked the nephew.

"He attacked the nephew violently, and the nephew ended up putting a good number of ax strikes to his head and it put an end to Napanin."

These are three of the stories that have built up the wendigo legend and made it so prominent in modern culture; so much so that I've even encountered people who claim a home is haunted by the very spirit said to possesses people and turn them into cannibals. I do not necessarily believe this to be true, but there's no doubting the power the word itself possesses.

Travelling to northwestern Alberta – do not worry you will hear all about it eventually – I was surprised by how many people believe the wendigo exists, especially when venturing outside urban centers into the vast plains and forests that make up most of the province. When one hears stories like the three that I have just recounted and revels in how gruesome and terrifying they are, it is not hard to understand why many believe them to be true – especially when all three cases are documented historically.

Before I share the details of my expedition, I think it's important to cover something already touched on in a previous chapter: the wendigo as a cautionary tale and how, more often than not, we are the monster.

The Monster is Us

When I was a young boy, I was fascinated – and more than a little frightened – by stories about monsters.

The first movie that ever really scared me is *The Beast Must Die*, a 1974 horror/mystery starring Calvin Lockhart and Peter Cushing. It is about a big-game hunter who invites a group of people to stay at his estate because he is convinced one of them is a werewolf. Think Agatha Christie's *Ten Little Indians* with a werewolf instead of a murderer.

Watching the movie as an adult, it is hard to believe it could scare anyone. But as a child of maybe eight, it was terrifying. The thought that you could be cursed and turned into a monster is frightening. The werewolf legend is in fact an allegory for the fragility of civilization's grip on the primal instincts of humanity. This idea stretches back all the way to ancient times when werewolf tales cautioned against people disrespecting the gods or, later in our history, questioning the church and religion. The werewolf is more than just a scary story: it is a cautionary tale.

My favorite fictional monster is Godzilla, who first rampaged across silver screens in the 1954 black-and-white

Japanese classic. By the time I discovered the colossal, fire-breathing monster in the 1970s he'd become a superhero of sorts, defending the Earth from a variety of creatures from the dark corners of both our planet and outer space. But, when he first emerged from the Pacific Ocean and stomped his way through Tokyo, he was something else entirely.

The original film came out just nine years after the United States detonated two atomic bombs over the Japanese cities of Hiroshima and Nagasaki, killing between 150,000 and 246,000 people and effectively leading to Japan surrendering to Allied forces at the end of the Second World War. This attack was still fresh in the Japanese people's minds. Godzilla was a created as a metaphor for nuclear weapons and the horrors they are capable of, a theme which resurfaced again in the 2023 release *Godzilla Minus One*.

Some have also suggested Godzilla is a metaphor for the United States. The nuclear strike against Japan was in retaliation for the bombing of Pearl Harbor on Sunday December 7, 1941. At the time, the United States was a neutral country in World War Two. This attack brought them into the Allied ranks. Godzilla was a giant beast awakened from its slumber by nuclear testing, who then takes a terrible vengeance on Japan.

Either way, Godzilla is a cautionary tale on the use of nuclear weapons and mankind's destructive nature.

Indigenous legends about wild men of the woods and lake monsters work much the same way. Stories about Sasquatch and Ogopogo are about respecting nature and the environment, otherwise it will turn on you. Trickster and Sasquatch legends caution about venturing deep into the woods at night for fear of being kidnapped and taken into another dimension. Good, scary fun, right? Well, sure. But it also serves as a warning against the dangers that potentially exist close by.

The wendigo legend is no different. The stories come from a time when, if people are starving in a village, hoarding food, or killing all the nearby animals so others cannot kill or eat them, they are behaving in a selfish way. The wendigo is then punishment for their actions.

"You wouldn't necessarily become a wendigo. You would act as wendigo. Wendigo is sort of a term rather than a name," explains Shearon.

The term wendigo was indeed originally used to describe a state of being rather than a specific creature. As stated earlier, the wendigo didn't appear as a physical creature until Algernon Blackwood's 1910 short story *The Wendigo*. Even in the stories covered in the previous chapter, Swift Runner and Napanin do not manifest into fifteen-feet-tall skeletal monsters with horns on their heads. They are people who believe they are becoming possessed by a being in the woods. In Swift Runner's case, this happens after he committed a horrible crime.

Shearon points out that people who hoarded food or even committed acts of cannibalism were not themselves described being wendigos but rather acting wendigo.

"It's the same with people who were starving and desperate and kill their neighbors and eat them…. they would be considered wendigo. They weren't acting like a wendigo, they are wendigo. That aspect of the Native culture I find really interesting because it has nothing to do with monsters. It's the monstrous behavior of people."

This behavior is referred to as Wendigo Psychosis, which is an endemic psychiatric disorder associated with culture, specifically the Algonquian people. People experiencing Wendigo Psychosis exhibit a range of symptoms including paranoia, anxiety, hallucinations and cannibalistic urges.

A paper published in the National Library of Medicine titled *Wendigo Psychosis and Psychiatric Perspectives of Cannibalism: A Complex Interplay of Culture, Psychology and History* takes a deep dive into the phenomenon. Its authors, Sean E. Oldak, Anthony J. Maristany, and Brianna C. Sa explore the implications of cannibalism within the realms of psychiatry, anthropology, psychology and sociology by navigating cultural beliefs, historical context, and psychological underpinnings.

Suffice to say it is a heady document, but Oldak, Maristany and Sa discovered that cannibalism is deeply ingrained in the cultural and mythological heritage of the Algonquian-speaking tribes. Therefore, it is closely associated with the wendigo, which is a symbolic figure the act.

"The wendigo serves as a warning about the potential loss of one's humanity in dire circumstances like starvation," they write.

The article states incidents of Wendigo Psychosis and cannibalism were more prevalent during times of extreme scarcity and famine among Algonquian tribes but also manifested in non-famine periods. The trio also found that cannibalism is often associated with psychiatric disorders but is not exclusively rooted in mental illness.

"Factors like substance abuse, antisocial traits and environmental upbringing can also contribute to cannibalistic acts. In some cases, cannibalism may be linked to survival instincts stemming from trauma and abuse," the article states.

The article also concludes the media's portrayal of cannibalism has an influence on public perception and cannot be underestimated.

Knudsen believes Wendigo Psychosis is the medical establishments attempt at "smashing" the wendigo subject into the Diagnostic and Statistical Manual of Mental Disorders, a handbook used by healthcare professionals in much of the world as an authoritative guide to the diagnosis of mental disorders.

"It's trying to get this into a relatable thing that we can diagnose and talk about," she explains. "It basically encompasses the entire subject of somebody turning wendigo; this insatiable hunger, wanting to eat human flesh, delusions, disrupted thinking. All of those things encompass Wendigo Psychosis."

According to Knudsen's research, there are three specific types of cannibalism, and the wendigo phenomenon falls into the category of pathological cannibalism, which accounts for the psychotic symptoms and delusional thinking that leads to the subject seeing family members as game animals or an entity entering a person's body and taking them over.

As with Oldak, Maristany, and Sa's findings, Knudsen states the psychosis is ethno-specific, as cases have only been recorded among Algonquin-speaking people.

"As far as I know there haven't been any cases of a Caucasian or African American people experiencing this," relates Knudsen. "This seems to be strictly within the Indigenous populations."

There are several theories within the medical communities as to what causes Wendigo Psychosis but none of these theories encompass every single case. This is why researchers like herself and friend Chad Lewis investigate the wendigo phenomenon on a case-by-case basis and why she believes the psychosis diagnosis is flawed.

One theory is famine and malnutrition cause people to go wendigo, as gut health has a lot to do with a person's mental health. Knudsen mentions one of the cures for being a wendigo is to drink bear grease or fats, which puts nutrients back into the body.

"The theory is that people are recovering from it because they are actually getting some nutrition at that point. However, the Swift Runner case blows this out of the water."

Swift Runner was not starving when he decided to kill and eat his family. Knudsen points out there was plenty of game present the winter when he claimed to be influenced by the wendigo. There was also no sign Swift Runner was starving, as he appeared to Father Lacombe to be healthy and well fed.

"Lumping everything together under Wendigo Psychosis isn't doing what's going on here justice."

She believes there is a tendency with researchers and the medical profession to lump things into physical or non-physical explanations when often these phenomena operate on a continuum between the two. To think otherwise is a mistake.

"In parapsychology, emotions, what we're projecting in our thoughts, how we are projecting consciousness, how we are receiving consciousness, all of that is intricate in no matter what we do… and I think this is the same. We can't just stick this [the wendigo] in one category. This is a little bit of both," argues Knudsen.

This is especially important to keep in mind when it comes to stories based on Indigenous folklore. Knudsen cites an interview she and *Supernatural Circumstances* co-host Michael Browne did with professor of folklore Lynne McNeill. McNeill said folklore can be true, it can be false, but it always gets something right. This attitude is important when approaching topics like the wendigo.

"There is something going on here and we have to be open minded and investigate it," asserts Knudsen.

A modern example of Wendigo Psychosis can be found in the case of Vince Li who, On July 30th, 2008, attacked, killed, and ate Tim McLean on a Greyhound bus travelling from Edmonton, Alberta, to Winnipeg, Manitoba. Witnesses said Li was sitting next to the sleeping McLean when he pulled a knife and began stabbing him in the neck and chest. The bus driver pulled to the side of the highway and all the passengers fled the vehicle. The driver and two other men tried to rescue McLean but were chased away by Li, who slashed at them and then locked the bus doors.

At this point, Li decapitated McLean and displayed his severed head through a window to those standing outside the bus. He then returned to McLean's body and began severing other parts and eating some of his flesh. This went on for several hours.

Li was arrested early the following morning when he attempted to flee the bus. Parts of McLean's body – his ear, nose and tongue – were found in plastic bags in Li's pockets.

Despite the gruesome nature of the crime, Li was found not criminally responsible for his actions as he was suffering from untreated schizophrenia when he attacked McLean. During the court case Li claimed a voice told him McLean was evil and had to be killed.

Carlson had recently written a story about the history of the wendigo that was published in an Edmonton newspaper. Knudsen states Li encountered this story prior to boarding the busy to Winnipeg.

"The connection Carlson had made was this incident may have been spurred on by this newspaper article," she argues. "Did his attention to the wendigo actually bring the wendigo to him and made him act out in this specific way? Nobody really knows."

De Jong agrees with Knudsen up to a point. He says the sheer volume of historical reports related to the wendigo give it credence. If it was one case or two, the phenomena could be dismissed as strictly psychological. But there are dozens of cases and even sightings of some… *thing* in the woods that fits the classical description of the creature.

"Is it real? Is it imagination? Or is it somewhere in-between?" he asks.

"If it wasn't for Jack Fiddler and all the actual legal documentation that's gone down for the last few centuries, I'd say it's just nonsense."

What prevents it from being "just nonsense" is the psychosis diagnosis, explains de Jong. If someone believed enough in the wendigo, then that belief could influence his or her actions.

"That just makes sense."

The medical community agrees, and, given Li's history of untreated mental illness, it seems likely this is a case of psychosis. But belief is a powerful thing, and many people do believe that simply uttering the wendigo's name can bring the spirit to your door. Given the wendigo story was born during a more uncivilized age, and cases of the wendigo occur in the barren landscape of rural Canada during the harshness of winter, it is not surprising such beliefs were born.

Ronald Murphy is a cryptozoologist, paranormal researcher, and author who penned *Lights in the Mist* for Small Town Monsters Publishing and appeared in the Small Town Monsters productions *Phantom Lights: UAPs of the Forest* and *UFOs Revisited*. He approaches high strangeness by looking at the psychological and sociological impact such phenomena and related archetypes have on people and society.

The wendigo has become one of these archetypes. Given the times and environment that the story was born in, it comes as no surprise to Murphy.

"These are locations that are not hospitable to people, especially in the wintertime," says Murphy, relating the wendigo to such folklore as the wild hunt.

The Wild Hunt is a motif occurring across various northern, western, and eastern European societies. It involves a chase led by a mythological figure escorted by a ghostly or supernatural group of hunters. To see the wild hunt is to forebode a catastrophe such as war or plague, or the death of the one who witnessed it. People who encounter the hunt might also be abducted into the underworld or the fairy kingdom.

While the specifics of the story are different, the meaning is very much the same, Murphy asserts.

"It's better not to be out and about in the wintertime because bad things can happen. The idea is taking these natural forces and personifying them into something else."

Due to its origins, wendigo is not only a point of interest to sociologists and anthropologists, but also to cryptozoologists as there seems to be a tangible, flesh-and-blood nature to it. Murphy argues one can approach the subject from a variety of ways, from true crime to possession to there being a real monster in the woods.

"Not only is it very fascinating but it's also multifaceted. There're so many different angles to come at it from."

Given her Indigenous heritage, Quill views the wendigo as very much a cautionary tale. Even when it comes to the actual sightings her *Coldspotters* team has investigated, the concept of the wendigo being a representation of the worst of humanity comes into play.

It is this sort of behavior that will attract an evil spirit like a wendigo or wraith to it and, in some cases, a haunting or possession can occur, she affirms. These are concepts and stories with which she was raised.

"What are these stories? If these stories are being told by our ancestors down through the years, there's a lesson there. There's something more that we need to be pulling from there."

As Shearon stated earlier, the wendigo would be associated with those who acted out of greed or gluttony during the frontier times. Quill argues the same lust for more holds true today, only now with the idea of addiction coming into play.

Drug addiction, a criminal lifestyle, and taking what isn't yours can all lead to someone "going wendigo", Quill explains.

"It's that poison within you. It's something that infests you to become that creature. That's something that's really important to know; those creatures are humans. They're just humans that have taken it too far."

Although most accounts depict Indigenous people as falling prey to the wendigo, anyone who lets greed take them over can "go wendigo." Quill is very much of the belief that the phenomena is a mix of the psychological and the physical.

"I think it's almost manifested into something. It was more of a story and a belief before and it's taken on a life of its own."

"Be careful what you ask for. That kind of thing."

She lives in Vancouver, where there is a lot of development. Once pristine waterfronts are being overrun with apartments and towers of glass and steel. Greenbelts are being clear cut with homes and businesses taking the place of trees. Waterways are being poisoned with sewage and other chemicals. Quill believes there is a price to pay for doing this to the environment and beings like the wendigo are here to collect.

"We're all that energy and it comes from Mother Earth. We're supposed to be taking care of that," she claims. "I think we need to slow down and take a look at what we're doing... We're messing with stuff that for tens of thousands of years kept us good and healthy, and now, within hundreds of years, we're completely and utterly falling apart."

When it comes to modern and Western society taking these stories and making them our own, Taylor believes it is important for media be respectful of their origins. Not only are we confusing different stories like the Skinwalker with the wendigo but also the point behind these tales is forgotten more often than not.

She states the wendigo began as an Indigenous fable told to children to prevent them from doing things that are thought to be taboo – things like succumbing to greed and cannibalism. That being said, Taylor is convinced the wendigo is real and roaming the woods of North America.

"I totally believe that they're running around out there. With my research I learned that you don't really die [as a wendigo]. You can starve out from hunger, but, alternately, you are this creature running around in the cold."

Murphy believes the multifaceted nature of the wendigo will make it an even more prominent figure in both pop culture and cryptozoological circles.

"It is such an adaptable figure. Bigfoot, you have the woods, but a Skinwalker, a wendigo, they can show up anywhere. They're duplicitous," he argues.

As he pointed out earlier, the creature's very origin speaks to the environment from which the stories have come. They are not just a cautionary tale about human behavior, but also about what dangers can befall us during the winter.

"What happens to the human mind whenever you are depleted of the natural resources in the wintertime?" Murphy asks.

"You would do things that you normally wouldn't do."

He cites stories of the Donner Party and the survival of the Uruguayan rugby team after their airplane crashed in the Andes mountains in 1972 as examples. In both cases people turned to cannibalism to survive harsh winter conditions.

"They had to essentially 'go wendigo' in order to live. That's a beastly thing. It's something we don't like to think about. It's one of those great taboos but, whenever push comes to shove, we do know in our human closets we do have a lot of skeletons."

If the wendigo is more than just a story, and if one possessed by a wendigo can conceivably wander the woods and plains indefinitely, then that would mean there's a chance – albeit a slim one – that an investigator could obtain physical evidence of such a creature.

One paranormal researcher jumped at the chance to do just that, and we're going to discuss this fascinating topic – and what his conclusions were – next.

Writing the Book on the Wendigo

If you are going to write a book about the wendigo, then you simply cannot do so without talking to Chad Lewis.

Lewis is a paranormal researcher, author, and lecturer with a master's degree in psychology. He's written twenty-five books on various aspects of high strangeness and has been featured on numerous television programs, including *Scariest Places on Earth*, *A Haunting*, and *Expedition X*.

In 2020 he and co-author Kevin Lee Nelson published the book *Wendigo Lore: Monsters, Myths and Madness*. It quickly became the go-to book on the subject as it explored all facets of the legend, including the regional and tribal differences. Lewis and Nelson even travelled to Alberta to experience the stories firsthand.

With that in mind and knowing I was doing something similar in terms of research, I had to talk wendigo with Lewis. Unfortunately, our collective schedules are busy enough that it took months to arrange a proper sit down where we could discuss all things wendigo. Once our schedules aligned, it became clear our conversation deserved its own chapter.

Lewis operates out of Minnesota, where the wendigo legend is almost as prevalent as it is in Western Canada. He spent the better part of fifteen years working on the book, having heard various stories about the wendigo while investigating and researching other topics. In fact, one such encounter he heard of in Northern Minnesota involved a strange light in the woods that accompanied an appearance by the creature – a fact that will become important later in this book!

"In Northern Minnesota it was thought to be a harbinger of death, like hearing the Irish banshee" Lewis says of the wendigo.

That tale got him started in his research. Growing up in the Great Lakes area of the United States, he and Nelson were fascinated by the story, having heard about the wendigo all their lives. But they found researching and writing the book was something that came and went in fits and starts.

"We'd start getting into it and say 'It's too big! It's too complex! It's too bizarre! We can't do it!' And then we'd put it on hold and pick it up six months later."

Each time they would start the book again the duo would feel they were not the right people to write it, he explains. They are white Caucasians, and the legend was an Indigenous one. He believes taking the amount of time it did to finish the volume made it better.

Whenever he would talk to people about the wendigo, he learned they discovered the story in one of three ways: through Marvel Comics as I did, via the television show *Supernatural,* or by way of the written works of William

Kent Kruger, a novelist and crime writer who featured the wendigo in several of his books.

Wendigo stories in the U.S., much like they are in Canada, started out as cautionary tales, but Lewis claims no matter how much he investigated this phenomenon, it quickly became clear that it is impossible to learn everything there is to know about it.

"I think the wendigo of four hundred plus years ago is different than the wendigo is today. There're so many variations. It's an indication of the white man clamping down in Canada on native Indigenous rights or the female role in the tribe."

He and Nelson avoided all that in their book due to the number of academic papers on the subject, even going so far as to avoid touching on Wendigo Psychosis, which we just discussed. Instead, the duo approached the subject from the stance that the wendigo is real and took the story from there.

A big part of his and Nelson's book involved travelling to Alberta and taking a boots-on-the-ground approach to researching the Swift Runner story. They chose to visit in the winter, when Canada in general and Northern Alberta in particular, can get very cold with conditions much like what Swift Runner would have experienced.

Even though his trip came a good hundred and fifty years after the Swift Runner case took place, not much had changed in terms of the environment, he speculates.

"It's still wide with thick forests. It's a place you would not want to be."

Lewis believes, and I agree, that one cannot write about a subject like the wendigo – or any other paranormal phenomena – without visiting where the activity or stories occur. Doing so allows the writer and researcher to, in essence, feel the story unfold.

He recalls being in Alberta within the rough area of where Swift Runner's camp had been in the Tawatinaw Valley. It hit him that Swift Runner's last remaining son would have been alive when Spring started, and that child had to have known he'd be the next to die.

"That fear of that just kind of hit me when I was there. I was just kind of overcome with emotion. I had been to a lot of serial-killer homes and… you think you're immune to it, but I wasn't expecting how hard it hit me standing there, putting myself in the shoes of that child."

Years later, and home safe in Wisconsin, when winter's chill hits, Lewis is transported back to the Tawatinaw Valley where perhaps the Swift Runner curse continues.

"It really affected me in a way that it never would have if I hadn't been there."

Lewis and Nelson visited Fort Saskatchewan and interviewed staff at the historical site about the Swift Runner case. They were especially curious about where he was eventually buried as there has been some disagreement on the exact location.

They also travelled to Slave Lake, a town of about six thousand people that is a three-hour drive north of Edmonton – a place Knudsen, Browne and I would also visit on our adventure – and Eating Creek: two places with notorious wendigo stories attached to them.

In modern terms, none of these locations are too far apart and are easily drivable. However, going back in time to the era of Swift Runner, much of the terrain and the geographical distance between sites would make travel daunting. This is especially true in the winter. Lewis said he and Nelson had a brand-new SUV fully equipped for winter driving and the proper clothing and equipment to survive in this hostile environment. Even then, being alone in this vast wilderness for too long would have placed them in danger.

Lewis explains many researchers have questioned why Swift Runner would resort to cannibalism when he could have trekked the twenty-seven miles to the nearest trading post for food and supplies.

"I don't think people realize that when you're malnourished for probably weeks, you're sick, you're dehydrated, you're weak as a dog; walking through waist-high snow is impossible. It may as well have been two thousand miles because he wasn't going to get there. Seeing the terrain. Seeing how thick and primitive the forest still is. Even in modern day, with all our technology and everything we had, we thought 'this could be dangerous out here if you're not prepared.'"

The Slave Lake incident is one with which I knew the least. I was aware, though, that I would be making the trek to that location soon enough, so I asked Lewis to explain the incident to me. He was happy to oblige.

In 1886, Marie Courtorielle had begun to display the classic signs of a possible wendigo possession. She had become aggressive, her body was swelling up, and she had begun seeing her friends and family as game animals.

Lewis explains some people believed Marie was going insane and that her husband, Michael, and son, Cecil, killed her to be done with her madness and blamed the incident on the wendigo story.

"They actually tried for many days and many nights using their best medicine and their best spirit on her but none of it worked."

This went on for three weeks. When Marie announced that she was going to kill them and became physically aggressive toward her husband and son, they were forced kill her.

"They buried her at the cemetery there. Everyone who knows anything about a wendigo knows you should burn it to crisp. I always joke that the grave's there, but is she still there?"

Indeed, the exact location of Marie Courtorielle's final resting place is unknown. There is even speculation that the body was dug up, moved to a different location, and burned.

Michael Courtorielle was convicted of murder and spent a year and a half to two years in prison. Lewis asserts the family acted out of mercy and fear and did not believe they were committing an act of murder.

As for Eating Creek, which is a remote, little developed area south of Slave Lake, the wendigo is viewed by some as a bit of folklore. Regardless of the hesitancy to believe the veracity of the tale, some people are leery about spending too much time there because of the story attached to the location.

"Even the white pioneers, the missionaries, they didn't want to go to it because it was a place where the wendigo resided," explains Lewis. "Two brothers who were thought to become wendigo, that was where they lurked."

What surprised Lewis and Nelson is most people in that part of Alberta knew of the Eating Creek story. Even if they did not believe it, they were aware of the wendigo and, in their own way, keeping the story alive.

Lewis and Nelson learned that people in Alberta take the wendigo seriously. Some even believe mentioning it can in some way summon the creature to you. He says it is almost like the wendigo is something that exists in the very atmosphere itself. Lewis has even had similar experiences when discussing the phenomena in his home state of Minnesota.

He was doing a lecture on mysterious creatures at a high school on a local reservation. Before his presentation, a couple of tribal elders approached him saying they knew he was going to discuss a creature from the area.

"We'd appreciate it if you didn't mention it at all. Don't talk about it. Don't mention it. Don't even allude to it."

Lewis was accommodating of the request, removing any mention of the wendigo from his program.

"My words had no sooner left my mouth and their body language just relaxed. They were terrified that I was going to talk about it."

Lewis states that he and Nelson soon made a point of not mentioning the wendigo to people during their trip to Northern Alberta, as they would often get perplexed responses from folks when they did ask questions. Some people – one journalist in particular – were willing to talk about the wendigo, but a lot of regular people were not.

"We got that a lot from both Indigenous and non-Indigenous people."

I had to inquire of Lewis, given the proliferation of wendigo stories within both Indigenous and Western culture, and the fact there are historical court cases and accompanying newspaper articles about people claiming to be influenced by such an entity during acts of murder and cannibalism, does he believe people fell victim to a psychosis or something very real that exists in the woods? Or did their culture's belief in the wendigo lead them to believe something was taking them over?

Lewis explains he struggled with this very question throughout researching and writing his book.

"When you have stories of people who heard a wendigo was in the vicinity – they didn't see it, they didn't hear it, they didn't feel it – they just heard it was somewhere coming; so, they stay in their lodging and starve to death rather than go out and look for food. That fear is real. If you're going to starve, or you're killing your grandmother or cousin because you think they're turning into a wendigo, regardless of what that means, your fear is real."

There are cases where people rendered a potential wendigo unconscious, stabbed them, ripped open their chest, and poured hot liquid onto the heart to melt it. Such an act was to stop the entity from completely taking control. Even then, the person was staked to the ground and decapitated for fear the wendigo would usurp the body.

"That kind of fear is real, so I struggled with the idea of was this all a mental illness. Was it just folklore that people took too seriously? Or was there something there?" he postulates.

Then, there is the physical element of people believing they saw this creature in the woods in the same way someone sees a bear. Lewis explains there are stories of tribal shamans conjuring the wendigo to do battle with it or send it after a rival tribe. The differing layers to this story can confuse the narrative.

Nelson likens the wendigo to a caterpillar transforming into a butterfly; it is ultimately the same thing through the entire process, but it is simultaneously new as well.

"Maybe the spirit of the wendigo is different than the flesh-and-blood animal."

Then there are the contradictions depending on where you are hearing the story. The wendigo is at times unkillable, but you can kill it. You can be cured of it, but once you consume human flesh you cannot be cured. Some legends say it can be killed by a silver bullet much like the werewolf. Lewis emphasizes the rules aren't cut and dry.

"I wrote this in the book that I feel like we were maybe a hundred years too late. That if we wrote it a hundred years ago there'd probably be some of those old original stories around. But when you're out in the woods starving, looking for a meal, you aren't writing down folklore," Lewis asserts.

To the people in the middle of these real-world narratives, the wendigo is as real as can be. They truly believe the entity is out there.

Rather than be frustrated by them, Lewis appreciates the various narratives and opinions about the wendigo. As far as he is concerned, there is no right or wrong answers as to what the wendigo is.

"I love hearing theories. I love hearing speculation. People come up to me and tell me what they think the wendigo is, and I never ever say 'oh that's wrong because I think it's this' because I have no idea."

He hopes more people will take an interest in the wendigo, research the stories, and write about them because there truly is so much material out there. Ultimately, he had some advice for me as I continued to do my deep dive into the material.

"Go with your instinct… because there's really no road map to this."

With that in mind, when the opportunity presented itself to go on an expedition to where the wendigo legend entered the public consciousness, I jumped at the chance.

Alberta Bound

To be honest, the wendigo came about during a period of malaise in my life. It was early 2024, and I was between projects. My previous collaboration with Small Town Monsters, the documentary *Cursed Waters: Creature of Lake Okanagan* and the accompanying book *The Legend of Ogopogo: Canada's Loch Ness Monster*, were pretty much complete and awaiting release at Monster Fest 2, which was still a few months away.

I had completed my post-production duties on the paranormal docuseries *We Want to Believe* and was counting down the days to my ghost hunting team's annual road trip to Gooding, Idaho. It is there that we partner with other investigators and explore a former tuberculosis clinic that is said to be haunted.

Professionally, I had time on my hands.

So, I sat down and started researching not one but two topics hoping they could jumpstart my creativity. One was the Cadborosaurus, a sea serpent that exists in the folklore of the Pacific Northwest and which has been sighted off the coast of Vancouver and Vancouver Island.

The other was the wendigo.

Both subjects fascinate me, and I would spend a day researching one cryptid and the next day diving into the other. I was unable to commit to one over the other. I was not sure what I would do with the information I had gathered. It was simply research for the sake of research.

One day I was on a video chat with Eli Watson, the director of *Cursed Waters: Creature of Lake Okanagan* among many other Small Town Monsters productions. Watson and I met during a promotional tour for *We Want to Believe*, when he interviewed me on his *Cryptid Campfire* podcast. During that conversation we became friends, kept in touch, and, for a time, I produced a video version of *Cryptid Campfire* for the *Paranormal Network*, a YouTube channel I managed for JoBlo Media.

In early 2023 I interviewed Watson for *Paranormality Magazine*. While we talked, he let me know the Small Town Monsters team was coming to Canada to shoot a documentary as part of the *On the Trail of Bigfoot* series. Watson had a few days to film a project of his own and he wanted to do something on Ogopogo, the lake monster believed to reside in Okanagan Lake. He asked me if I wanted to be a part of the project and the rest is history.

Our conversation in 2024 was about how post-production was going on *Cursed Waters*. At the time, the project was basically complete save for a few minor changes and tweaks. The discussion quickly shifted to our next favorite topic – which Lego set we were currently building – when out of the blue he asked me "so what book are you writing next?"

For one of the few times in my life I wasn't sure what to say. Then it popped out of me; "the wendigo."

"Dude, you need to talk to Heather! We're making a movie about the wendigo next year and I'm directing it."

Heather is, of course, Heather Moser, a producer and researcher for Small Town Monsters and the editor for Small Town Monsters Publishing. When I texted her about the wendigo book idea, we had a quick phone chat and before I knew it, I was unofficially working on my next book for Small Town Monsters Publishing and involved in a wendigo documentary, for which the book would be a companion piece!

By this time, I had also contacted Knudsen, who I knew through our mutual paranormal contacts. Being Canadian, and there not being a huge number of Canadian paranormal researchers and investigators, we had crossed paths online but never met face-to-face. She lives in Edmonton in northcentral Alberta, where a lot of wendigo stories originate.

Knowing the project was now more than simple research, I reached out to her. I asked if she would be interested in a formal interview on the subject. Little did I know I was about to tap into a gold mine of information.

Not only was Knudsen familiar with the subject, but also, she lives in close vicinity to where much of the Swift Runner case occurred, including Fort Saskatchewan where he was hanged. We agreed to arrange a video call to discuss next steps.

That call ended up involving Michael Browne, Knudsen's *Supernatural Circumstances* co-host and true-crime podcaster. During that meeting it became very clear to me that a trip to Edmonton, and then a tour of the sites associated with Swift Runner and other wendigo encounters, was required.

This included a documented wendigo possession case. In addition, we would delve into an encounter Knudsen believes she and others had with the creature at a location outside of Edmonton called Ma-Me-O Beach in August of 2023.

On the spot I decided I not only needed to go to Edmonton but document the experience on video: film the interview and on-the-ground encounters as if I were making a documentary of my own. If the footage worked for the wendigo documentary, great. If not, at least I would have captured all the elements – visual, audio and emotional – to properly convey this phenomenon.

Fortunately, Browne was a student of film as well and would be able to shoot footage for me and capture clean audio with equipment of his own.

I arranged some potential dates with Knudsen and Browne, confirmed this was also okay with my long-suffering and supportive wife, and a plan was set: I would travel to Alberta for five days in May… little more than a week after returning from the expedition to Gooding, Idaho.

This plan set in stone, I shifted focus to the Gooding trip as it would be two long travel days and four full days of investigating and documenting paranormal activity. My colleagues Pete Renn, Olivier Asselin, and I would be living in this haunted location and working almost twenty-four hours a day. On top of two fifteen-hour commutes from Canada to Idaho, the trip would be emotionally and physically demanding.

Suffice to say, I was completely spent when I returned home and immediately fell into a deep, depressive funk. I occasionally struggle with depression and fell into another episode the day after returning from Gooding. The last thing I wanted to do was travel again. I just wanted to stay home with my wife and son.

But plans had been put in motion, and, following another meeting with Knudsen and Browne, I felt more invigorated for this next adventure. We had planned my time in Edmonton to the letter, setting aside the first day for formal interviews and a night venture out to Ma-Me-O Beach to investigate the alleged wendigo encounter. Day two would be the first leg of tracking the Swift Runner story, including stops in the Tawatinaw Valley where he murdered and ate his family, as well as travelling north to Slave Lake and Eating Creek, where two other wendigo tales are set. The third and final day would be the second half of Swift Runner's journey and would conclude at Fort Saskatchewan, where he was held and eventually executed.

The days would be full, and I would be without my usual collaborators. Regardless, I was looking forward to meeting and working with Knudsen and Browne while digging deeper into wendigo folklore. To be on the ground following the case that really started it all would be exciting and bring the story alive.

There were nine days between the Gooding trip and my adventure in Alberta, and I made the most of my time with my family and rested up as much as possible between researching the wendigo and preparing for the trip. I was oddly apprehensive about going but also excited for this new adventure.

Then, on the night before I left, my son called me into his room for a second time after going to bed, something he does not usually do. He was crying, which was also unusual.

"What's wrong buddy?"

"I don't want you to go! I'm afraid something bad is going to happen."

I rubbed his back, kissed him on the top of his head, and held him a while, something I had not done since he was six or seven years old.

I whispered him some assurances:

"It's going to be okay. I'll be home before you know it. Nothing bad is going to happen. I'll be fine."

I continued to hold him until he fell asleep and then went downstairs to watch television for a bit. I tried to relax, but my son's sadness made it difficult. The next morning, I woke up, finished packing, and prepared to leave. What enthusiasm I had for the trip, though, had drained from me. Was being away twice in one month too much? Was I doing the right thing by my family?

My wife, who is the logical one in our household, reminded me our son's anxiety does get the better of him from time to time. She also emphasized that once I arrived in Edmonton and things get rolling, I would surely be caught up in the expedition. Now it was her turn to whisper assurances to me:

"Griffon will be fine. I'll be fine. You'll be fine. You need to do this. It's what you do."

We hugged and kissed, I packed up the truck, gave my son the biggest hug ever, and went out the door.

"See you both in four days. Love you," I said and left.

The drive from my hometown of Kamloops to Edmonton is just shy of nine hours and a lot of the drive is on a windy, two-lane highway…at least until one enters Alberta. The scenery, however, is some of the best you will ever see in the world…at least until one enters Alberta.

Sorry. That is a bit of a joke. British Columbia is made up of vast forests and herculean mountains, especially along the Rocky Mountain Range that borders the two provinces. The views are comparable to what people see in Alaska or the Pacific Northwest, with jagged, snow-covered peaks poking out of lush greenbelts. The trip can be truly breathtaking at times.

I stopped in Jasper for lunch. Jasper is a tourist town in the heart of Jasper National Park and a little more than halfway between Kamloops and Edmonton. It has world-class restaurants, skiing and snowboarding, and sightseeing. There are also ample opportunities to view wildlife like moose, bear, and deer. Sadly, the town was threatened by a large forest fire months after my stop and parts of the community have been literally burned from the map.

Once clear of the Rocky Mountains, the land flattens into the prairie region of Canada. The joke amongst motorists is that one can put a brick on the gas, tie the steering wheel so it doesn't turn, and fall asleep. The car will continue a straight line for days without needing to turn.

The scenery also changes. There are stands of trees and forest but dispersed across flat and at times rolling grasslands. This is broken up by the occasional river, lake, city or town. There is not much to look at and you can see for miles. This is not to say Alberta isn't beautiful in its own way, but it is most definitely not British Columbia.

That is, you could see for miles if the sky was not socked in with smoke. To the north of Edmonton, a large forest fire burned near the community of Fort McMurray and the smoke had drifted down to Edmonton, limiting visibility and turning the sky an ominous reddish grey. Forest fires are sadly a regular occurrence in British Columbia during the summer, and communities are smothered with smoke for days on end. This often forces people to stay indoors. All of this combined darkened my mood even more.

Miles and hours ticked by and Google Maps eventually let me know I was nearing the turnoff to my hotel, which I had booked in West Edmonton as that was closest to where Knudsen lives. It seemed a good base of operations to work from for the next few days. I followed directions to my hotel, and, pulling up, my heart sank even more.

Booking a hotel online can be tricky, and I had a hard time picking a place to stay. I finally settled on one and had hoped for the best. Pulling in, however, it was clear to me that settling on a hotel on the fringe of the city was not my best call. The neighborhood was questionable, there were homeless people scattered everywhere, and a security guard at the door. Also, what appeared to be a new and clean establishment from the website pictures was anything but.

Exhausted, I booked myself in and hauled my suitcases and equipment to my room. I was just walking through the door when Knudsen texted me. Browne had arrived at this hotel, and his room was too dark and noisy to conduct our interviews the next day. Would mine suffice? I snapped a few quick pictures and sent them to her. We agreed that, although small, my room would work.

One battle won, the rest of the first night was spent unpacking and finding a restaurant for dinner, as I was starving. A decent bottle of whisky was also appreciated. I tried relaxing in the hotel pool – one of the reasons I gravitated toward this hotel in the first place, but the cheap rates meant a lot of families had chosen this place as an affordable weekend getaway. There was barely any room to sit, let alone swim.

Tired and more than a little disappointed I retreated to my room for a nightcap and some sleep. The next day was going to be busy.

The Hunt Begins

Although the skies were still filled with smoke, the world looked much better the following morning. It was a Sunday.

I ate a quick breakfast in the hotel restaurant and contacted Knudsen and Browne. It was agreed that I would pick her up at her place, which was a short ten-minute drive from my hotel. From there, we would meet Browne at West Edmonton Mall, which was across the street from his hotel.

For the uninitiated, West Edmonton Mall is alleged to be North America's largest shopping mall. It's 5.3 million square feet in size, has twelve worldclass tourist attractions including a skating rink, water park, amusement park, dozens of restaurants, two hotels, and more than eight hundred stores. There is enough parking for thirty thousand people. Essentially, it is a little city unto itself.

We figured this would be a great place to meet, grab a quick lunch, and then venture back to my hotel to conduct our interviews for the day. In addition to Knudsen, I would interview Alisia Perrault-Werner, her husband Darrick Werner, and their daughter Willow Werner about the wendigo encounter they believe they had the previous

August. The plan was also to venture that evening to Ma-Me-O Beach where the encounter took place.

Being able to follow the Swift Runner story was one thing, and I was excited for the opportunity. But to interview people about a modern wendigo sighting and visit where it happened – and potentially encounter one of these creatures – made this whole trip truly worthwhile.

The first order of business was to pick up Knudsen. I was anxious to meet her. Not because I doubted that we would hit it off, as every video conversation we had so far went smoothly, but because we had never actually worked together before. Fortunately, any doubts I had were quickly erased as she walked to my truck with bags of audio and video equipment in hand. I recognized her immediately, not only from our conversations, but also having watched her appearances on *Paranormal 911*.

We greeted each other with a quick hug, and I helped her load her bags into the back of my truck. Our conversation on the drive to the mall was quick and breezy, like we had been friends for years. We talked mostly about anything but the adventure we were about to embark on.

Knudsen directed me to a decent parking spot at the mall, and we messaged Browne, asking him to meet us at the Lego Store. It was here that I hoped to pick up gifts for my wife and son [and a little something for myself]. We are, after all, a family of Lego builders, us Hewletts.

Now that we were on the ground and ready to get to work, my depressed mood began to lift. I was still fatigued but also energized by the prospect of doing what I love to do. Knudsen is an enthusiastic presence, clearly loving the world of high strangeness as much as I do.

We discussed plans for the day, with the Perrault-Werner clan meeting us at my hotel room early that afternoon while we waited for Browne amongst a crowd of other would-be Lego purchasers outside the store.

"There he is," Knudsen said and pointed at Browne as he made his way towards us. Browne is short and a bit stocky with a mustache and glasses. In addition to being Knudsen's co-host on *Supernatural Circumstances* he is also the host of *Dark Poutine*, a Canadian true-crime podcast. Adding to his resume, he is also the author of two books; *Murder, Madness and Mayhem: Twenty-Five Tales of True Crime and Dark History* and *Strange, Spooky and Supernatural.*

There was something familiar about Browne that I could not put my finger on. I thought it was because we had spoken online a few times, and I was feeling a little tired from the drive the previous day. We shook hands as the Lego store opened and quickly went inside.

I will not bore you with the details of what happened inside the store. Suffice to say more money was spent than necessary. More importantly, I regret nothing!

We grabbed lunch and then drove to my hotel to set up for our series of interviews. We beat the Perrault-Werner family by a matter of minutes, and, after quick introductions were made, Browne and I finished setting up our cameras and audio equipment for what would be the expedition's formal interviews.

Knudsen was first up, and you have already read some of what we discussed during her interview. The rest shall be revealed at various points throughout the remainder of this book.

Next up was Alisia Perrault-Werner, who revealed she was introduced to the wendigo phenomena through her Indigenous heritage.

"There's a lot of folklore and oral history around wendigo. Generally speaking, we're not supposed to talk about it or engage with it. It's something that is dangerous for humans just to be around, so we try to avoid it at all costs."

This was news to me, although I would speak with many people in the paranormal community after this expedition who would support what Perrault-Werner said. Merely speaking the word could potentially put you in the wendigo's path, not unlike summoning Bloody Mary, which is a folk story in its own right.

Perrault-Werner continued, saying she once tried talking about wendigo with her uncle, which made him visibly uncomfortable. Even being pressed as to what could happen if the wendigo is mentioned is taboo.

"You just don't talk about it."

Based on what she has heard culturally, the wendigo prays on people who are unwell or are, as she puts it, "vibrating on a different frequency."

"It preys on desperation. If you're not in a good mind space it can definitely prey on how you're feeling and make you do unkind things to others."

Reiterating what Knudsen said earlier in the book, Perrault-Werner believes the wendigo is a combination of physical and non-physical phenomena. She said her encounter with what she believes is a wendigo supports this.

"I don't know if what I saw was physical, but I was able to see it, so I think it has components of both."

There was no hesitation on her part when it came to explaining this encounter. Perrault-Werner explained she and her family had become close friends with Knudsen and have joined her on several paranormal adventures. On the evening of their encounter, the group of investigators had received a tip that they should check out the Ma-Me-O Beach area, which is a summer village about one-hundred kilometers (sixty-two miles) south of Edmonton. The land is also traditional territory for the Cree people.

The tip explained that venturing to Ma-Me-O Beach could result in a Dogman sighting. Being up for pretty much any kind of adventure, the team ventured out that summer evening.

"I think we left town around ten and made it to Ma-Me-O Beach around eleven."

If you're not familiar with Dogman or related phenomena I highly recommend you check out my friend and colleague Aaron Deese's books *The Texas Dogman Triangle* and *Hunting Grounds: Dogmen of the Lakes* from Small Town Monsters Publishing. Deese is as close to an expert as one can get on the subject, and his books are a great resource.

The idea of seeing a Dogman did not deter anyone in the group. They believe they had seen such creatures in the area around Edmonton before.

Knudsen, Perrault-Werner, and her family drove the long straight roads and side roads to Ma-Me-O Beach, which is when the evening took a spooky and mysterious turn.

"As we were driving out to Ma-Me-O Beach there was some intense mist and fog along the journey. You couldn't see the road beside you."

The mist would move and almost corral the vehicle along the road and side roads. Almost like the mist was leading them somewhere.

"Whether or not it was, that's how it felt to us. We'd get to certain parts, and the mist would be gone but we somehow felt this wasn't the right place, so we followed the mist."

Willow described the fog as the weirdest fog she had ever seen. It did not even move like regular fog.

"It wouldn't move with the truck as we were driving," Willow recalls.

"I'd roll down the window and it was like a wall of fog beside us."

Wanting to pay her respects, the group parked on the side of a road near Ma-Me-O Beach and Perrault-Werner started the evening off with a smudge with the intention to bring positive energy to the adventure. Smudging is an Indigenous cultural practice that involves burning plants for the purpose of cleansing and purifying oneself, a space, or an object.

The ceremony complete, Knudsen, Perrault-Werner, and her family drove further into the Ma-Me-O Beach area. It was here that the mist returned, guiding them on some seemingly predetermined route. They had been to the region before but now found themselves in a place with which they were unfamiliar.

"We'd come to a fork in the road. Do we go left? Do we go right? We'd go right because the mist is thicker," Perrault-Werner recalls.

They eventually reached a crossroads, and it just felt right to stop. Darrick Werner parked the truck, the headlights facing a field. Behind them was a road and behind the road was a stand of thick trees.

Everyone got out of the vehicle and stood on the side of the road, focused on the open field before them. Sitting quietly, they eventually heard the distinct yip of coyotes in the distance.

"Sometimes, when you hear coyotes, it means Dogman is in the area," she emphasizes.

"We could hear the yipping, so we were focused on that area for quite some time."

The yipping eventually died down, leaving the group in the dark, standing in silence. It was then that they saw the light shine through the forest behind them.

The light was bright and formed in such a way that it looked like a tunnel. Although, at the time no one was sure exactly what they were looking at nor understood why the light was there.

Willow recalls that the trees moved, almost like they were opening to form a tunnel for the light.

"It was almost as if there was a spotlight and nothing in it," she explains.

Then a figure appeared in the light. Something thin and oddly shaped. At first, it almost seemed like a tree or something static.

"I kept looking, trying to make out what it was, and it almost looked like it had arms. I was like 'what is that?'"

It moved, prompting Knudsen to tell everyone they should get back in truck. There was a need to have something – anything – between them and the figure moving in their direction.

"When Morgan Knudsen says get in the truck, you get in the truck."

At first, Knudsen thought the light was coming from a house recessed back through the trees or someone walking towards them with a lamp or flashlight in hand. It soon became clear to her there was no home there in the woods or person moving behind the light. It continued to expand the longer they looked at it.

The figure in the light was backlit and therefore appeared to be solid black. Its head was lowered, and its limbs and body were thin and skeletal. The arms were raised in an upside-down cactus shape.

"We had the feeling it was looking at us; that it could see us. I started to realize we don't know what this is and here we are standing out on the side of the road. So, I said 'let's get in the car, get in truck. We gotta put something between us and whatever this is because I don't know what it is,'" Knudsen relates.

Everyone got into the truck and watched as the shape turned as stiffly as it had first moved and walked back into the light.

Then the light collapsed into itself and both it and the dark, thin shape were gone.

Darrick Werner did not see the shadow figure in the light. He said his attention was on the light itself, which seemed to have no specific point of origin.

"You couldn't tell the source of the light, yet it [was clear that it] wasn't that far away. It just lit up everything in the general direction toward us."

He could see a clear path through the trees toward them and the underbrush lit from behind. He racked his brain

74

trying to figure out what the light was and where it came from. Was it from a house or a vehicle? Werner couldn't figure it out.

Once everyone was back in his truck, Werner backed the vehicle up and turned it so that the headlights faced where the light, which was now gone, had been. All they could see was thick brush and trees and a telephone pole where the light had been just moments before. There was nothing there which could have caused the light they all saw.

Those trees, brush, and the telephone pole were not visible when the light was present.

"It was something interesting to see for sure," Werner says, adding he has no idea what it was they saw.

He hoped the light could have come from a house set back in the woods, but the trees and brush were too thick for that to be possible. Any house lights they did see were barely visible that night. This light, in contrast, was extremely luminous.

"You could see the bright light very clearly, and there was no tree between us and whatever that source of light was from."

Knudsen hypothesized that the group might have witnessed something coming through a portal.

Portals are a key element in paranormal lore and represent openings that connect other worlds, eras, and realms of existence to ours. There are many theories about what they are and how they work – enough to fill an entire volume of its own. When it comes to beings like Sasquatch there is a strong belief, especially among Indigenous people, that these creatures are dimension walkers and use portals to move between our world and the spirit realm.

Perrault-Werner wondered if wendigo, or whatever it is they saw that night, does the same?

"With Indigenous oral tradition we talk about Mother Nature and water and the land and how that's a connection. Is that traditional territory [Ma-Me-O Beach] a part of how these beings are able to transport themselves? I'm not sure."

Everyone kept an eye out for the light in case it reappeared on the drive home, but it never did. Willow said the whole experience just did not feel right.

"We were all in shock talking about it. It was just like utter confusion and utter shock."

Perrault-Werner said the encounter – especially the figure seen in the light – frightened her: a sensation she does not usually associate with paranormal phenomena.

"Definitely that feeling, and the fear that I felt, that was new to me. It tells me it's something we shouldn't be messing around with," she emphasizes.

She noticed as well that each streetlight they passed under would quickly flicker out as they passed beneath it, only to flicker back on afterward.

"It just added a whole other level of strangeness to the whole night."

This encounter intrigued me. For one, all four people involved in the experience relayed it the same, which is a rare occurrence. As a crime journalist, I interviewed hundreds of people about murders, fires, accidents – you name it. Most of the time there was some variation in the story. This does not indicate someone is lying, but we all interpret things differently, and, as a result, witness accounts come out differently depending on who is doing the explaining.

Knudsen and all three members of the Perrault-Werner clan explained the exact same sequence of events in similar fashion. Only Darrick's was different, but that is because he was focused on the light more than what the others saw in it. Either this was a well-coordinated story or the truth, and I trust Knudsen and her reputation so, by default, I trust the others. That only leaves one card left on the table.

As for the portal concept – I was skeptical about the idea until science started delving into multiverse theory, which hypothesizes that there are many universes and ours is just one of them. These universes all exist at the same time. In paranormal terms, this could explain the existence of ghosts, cryptids, unidentified flying objects and where they come from – another universe existing side by side with ours. For them to reach our world there would need to be a doorway of some kind, and that is where portals come into play.

Reading the works of John Keel, who wrote *The Mothman Prophecies* among many other volumes about high strangeness, and Colm A Kelleher's exploration of the Skinwalker Ranch phenomenon with *Hunt for the Skinwalker: Science Confronts the Unexplained at a Remote Ranch in Utah*, I've been more swayed toward accepting the existence of portals. Not to mention many Indigenous cultures believe in portals as well. Who am I to argue with them?

Our interviews concluded, we bid farewell to the Perrault-Werner family, arranging to meet them after dinner for our expedition to Ma-Me-O Beach. My excitement for this adventure was heightened even more after hearing about the encounter they had.

The rest of the day was spent touring Edmonton with Knudsen and Browne and getting to know them.

There were a few times during our walking tour of parts of Alberta where we had to pause and rest for Browne, who was experiencing painful stomach issues. He assured us this was not uncommon for him, at least lately, and was something he was getting looked at back home in Vancouver.

As the hours passed, I felt like I was making new friends, which is not always the case with me. The feeling that I knew Browne from somewhere other than his books and podcasts was growing.

However, my focus was on the night ahead and my desire to capture some kind of evidence that the wendigo existed beyond the realm of folklore. Little did I know what the evening had in store.

Ma-Me-O Beach

One thing that quickly became clear about driving in Alberta is just because something looks close on a map, does not make it so.

Ma-Me-O Beach seemed like a hop, skip, and a jump away from Edmonton. In reality, though, it is a good hour-long drive along the extended, straight stretches of highway and road that crisscross the entire province. Knudsen, Browne, and I followed the Perrault-Werners in my truck. Keeping up with Werner, who drove his pickup like a Formula 1 car, was a little tricky but I managed to stay close behind them.

The forest fire smoke lingered in the air but had thinned somewhat. Knudsen said the forecast called for the smoke to be gone by the following day, which was great news as we were scheduled to spend it on the road tracking the Swift Runner locations.

Our route eventually took us off the highway onto a series of backroads that seemed to stretch out forever in one long direction. There was the occasional turn onto another straight line, but it was nothing reminiscent of the sharp and winding curves that accompany navigating roads back home.

All around us was grassland which, in most places, was still brown in color with only a bit of green sprouting up as the vegetation came back to life. Thick clumps of forest stood as well, the leaves just starting to spring forth.

Knudsen pointed out where the strange mist had started to appear the previous August. To experience such a thing, in the dark especially, would be eerie. Even though other vehicles passed us, and we did pass farms and homesteads from time to time, it felt very much isolated here.

We eventually arrived at our destination. It was a road leading to a gated property on the side of the route that we had been travelling on for a while. Werner parked, his front end facing across the road toward the stand of trees where, months ago, they had seen *something*. I pulled in behind him, and everyone exited their respective vehicles.

While studying the location where a portal of light had appeared weeks earlier, it became immediately clear there was nothing that could have caused such an illumination to manifest. All that existed across the road was a thick stand of trees and the power pole, which stood beside the entrance to a secondary road. I guessed that this road must lead to the home where Werner described seeing a faint light.

We stood and stared, vehicles passing by us from time to time.

"I remember exactly where it is," said Willow, looking across the road to where the form appeared.

"Yup, there it is," Perrault-Werner replied.

"There's nothing. Just solid trees."

"I could've sworn it was just a hollow thing in the trees," Willow continued.

"It's so strange," added Knudsen.

The three women stood in silence for a moment before Knudsen pointed off toward the southeast, revealing another expanse of flatland with more stands of trees in the distance. This was all behind the gate and barbed wire fence.

"We heard the coyote right over this way," Knudsen explained before turning and stepping a few feet over to the west, near the edge of the side road.

"And we were standing right over here."

By now Browne had appeared with some microphones we planned to use for recording the roadside interview along with any pertinent comments that might be said while exploring the area. The plan was to eventually move on from here to the beach itself and to wait there until dark, hopefully having another encounter.

Perrault-Werner would lead us through a smudge ceremony to protect the group from any negative energy we might experience. One microphone was attached to her, the other to Knudsen. While Perrault-Werner gathered what she needed for the smudge, Knudsen explained we now stood alongside an average country road in Alberta: one where no one would expect to experience the surprise of their lives.

"As you look across the road here, you can see a solid bank of trees. There's simply no tunnel, there's no light, there's nothing. There's not even a spot for a light to shine through."

"This isn't a walking area. There's nobody down here. This isn't even a good place to be stopping as there's traffic flying past."

On cue a red pickup sped by us.

Knudsen stated it was pitch dark when the encounter occurred. We, however, were still a short time away from sunset. Going over the events one more time, she said it was one of the strangest things she has ever experienced in her career as an investigator.

Then Perrault-Werner appeared with a wooden box in hand. The contents included a feather, sage, and other materials she intended to use for the smudge. She explained that as the sage would be burned, the smoke would spread over each one of us. During this, she would recite a prayer in both Cree and English.

"It's to start our evening off in a good way and to make sure we are carrying on with good intentions and seeing things with clear eyes, speaking with kind words, and really just paying respect to Mother Nature, to each other, and to those that we may encounter tonight."

In addition to the smudge, we would also make an offering of tobacco, which is the first medicine of Indigenous people. This would be done out of thanks and reciprocity to the Earth and to any physical or non-physical beings we might encounter that evening.

"So, we're giving and not just taking from anything we meet here tonight."

The smudge would not only be done at the beginning of the night, but also at the end as well to clean away any negative energies we may have encountered before returning home.

It took a few matches for Perrault-Werner to light the sage, creating a waft of smoke she stoked by waving her feather and blowing gently with her lips. She was ready to start the prayer.

"We ask that you join us and bless this Earth, and we ask that this smoke and this smudge be carried to you to carry our prayers tonight."

She continued, asking for the evening to start in a good way and for us to remain open to whatever would be shown to us. She also acknowledged we were on the traditional land of the Cree and Metis people and that we would respect any living and non-living entities in the area.

"We're just here to learn and ask that you show us in a gentle way."

The prayer concluded, Perrault-Werner asked each of us to come forward in turn, cupping the smoke with our hands, essentially "washing" it over ourselves as if we were splashing our heads, faces, and bodies with water.

When it was my turn, Perrault-Werner explained bringing the smoke to my eyes would allow me to see the world clearly. Waving it across my ears would help me to hear with clear intentions. Washing it over my mouth aided me in speaking with kind words. I brought some to my heart, setting a positive intention before pulling the smoke over my head and down the rest of my body, completing my part of the smudge.

Once everyone had completed the smudge we walked across the road to where the tunnel of light had appeared, something Knudsen and the Perrault-Werner clan had not had the opportunity to do that fateful night. Perrault-Werner encouraged us to move across the road.

"Let's just go down in the ditch here where we saw it."

She continued to stoke the smudge and spread the sage smoke with her feather to effectively cleanse the area around us.

We all spread out and explored different sections of the roadside. I followed Willow

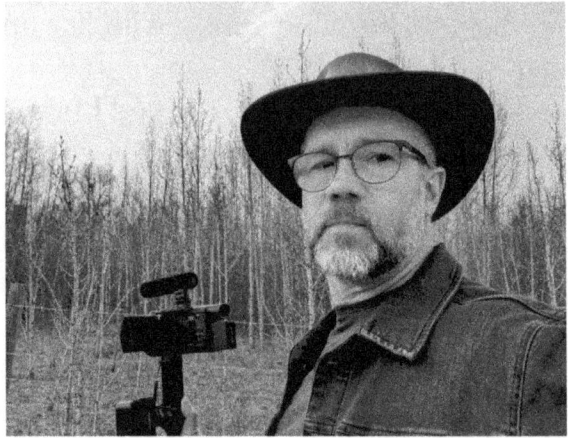
Author at Ma-Me-O Beach Site

and Perrault-Werner to the fence while Knudsen, Werner, and Browne hung back by the road. Perrault-Werner then said another prayer, first in Cree and then English, offering tobacco in honor of the land and physical and non-physical beings in the area. The prayer completed, Willow spread the tobacco leaves on the ground as an offering.

I was struck by how barren the area looked. Even the trees were akin to tall, brown skeletons void of life. I saw nothing in the immediate area that could have produced, or even reflected, the kind of light Knudsen and her friends saw that night. There were trees – a lot of trees – the fence and a power pole. Nothing more.

"So, Darrick, that was the pole you ended up seeing when you turned the vehicle around?"

He moved toward the power pole. I followed. He began to recount his memories from that night.

"When the light was pole, but as soon as I turned the truck around and the light dissipated, you could see that pole very clearly."

He pointed to the road beside the power pole and said they knew the road was there. Other than that, there was nothing else aside from forest. There was nothing that could cause any illumination.

"There's a house back there and you could see the lights on the house, but they were tiny little pinpricks of light like what you'd see in the distance."

"There's another house off the east of us, but it's set back and nowhere near where the tunnel of light appeared."

The main road along which we had been traveling as well as the side road by the power pole lead to the beach, which was the next location on our agenda.

With sun starting to set, a faint red glow was cast due to the forest-fire smoke that hung in the sky. Visible through the barren branches of the forest, it set an ominous mood. Somewhere a flock of Canada Geese honked as they flew by.

Knudsen suggested we drive on to the beach and wait for the sun to go down, then we could return to this spot closer to the time of the encounter – eleven thirty – and see if we could witness a repeat performance. Everyone agreed. We headed back to our respective vehicles.

Knudsen, Browne, and I followed the Perrault-Werners down the side road toward the beach. Another thick stand of trees was to the west of us. To the east was the forest where the tunnel of light had manifested. These woods eventually gave way to a clearing where one of the houses Werner described stood, along with a small outbuilding or two.

Then, we saw the cemetery. How interesting.

Knudsen exclaimed and immediately dialed Perrault-Werner on her phone. Browne trained his GoPro on the rows of white crosses as we drove past.

"What the hell?!" she said into her phone. Then, in response to something Perrault-Werner must have said on the other end:

"Oh, we're seeing it!"

"It's Native, isn't it?" Browne asked.

I tried to focus on the road during all of this. I had no desire to drive into Werner's truck ahead of us or even off into the trees. Even so, I also tried taking in the cemetery, which was the size of a small field.

Knudsen turned to Browne and me from the passenger's seat, her phone still in her hand:

"Alisia said it's a traditional burial ground."

Browne pointed out the burial ground rests in an almost straight line with where Knudsen and the Perrault-Werner family saw their tunnel of light.

"I'm, like, shook right now," Perrault-Werner said through the speakers of Knudsen's phone.

"I wasn't expecting that."

"That makes sense you'd have that experience just twenty meters away from that [burial ground]," said Browne.

Perrault-Werner, her voice having a noticeable shake to it, "One hundred percent. One hundred percent."

There is a long-standing trope in popular culture about the Indigenous burial ground being a cause for hauntings and other supernatural events. Movies and books like *The Amityville Horror*, *The Shining* and *Pet Sematary* cemented this notion in modern audiences. Years later, alleged reality television shows like *Ghost Adventures* would lead viewers to believe the spirits of those buried in said burial grounds are to blame for demonic activity.

As is often the case, these ideas are based in folklore, and, as it quickly became clear to me, Indigenous people like Perrault-Werner and investigators such as Knudsen take the concept seriously. They do not equate burial grounds with hauntings and demonic activity.

In fact, Perrault-Werner stated each Indigenous nation has their own teachings about burial grounds. Such teachings are passed down by an elder, but she has not received such teachings. Therefore, she could not speak to her nations' philosophy about burial grounds.

We found a spot to pull over and gather beside our vehicles. Knudsen and Perrault-Werner were visibly blown away, for lack of a better word, by what we had just seen.

"We didn't know anything about what was behind those trees. We couldn't even see a road around because it was just so dark here. It was crazy," Knudsen recalled of the August encounter.

No one knew the cemetery/burial ground was there at that time.

Perrault-Werner explained more about the location where we were standing. We were on the Pigeon Lake Reserve, land shared by four First Nations in the province of Alberta. She reiterated that fact alone establishes the cemetery as a traditional burial ground. She was nearly speechless, but also a little excited.

"It kind of gives more credibility to what we saw that night. That it was something special."

Pausing here for a moment, I want to return to my conversation with Ronald Murphy. During a discussion with him, I brought up the idea of burial grounds so that I could get his insight on the matter. He said graveyards, especially Indigenous graveyards, are a common location for Dogman sightings. Knudsen and company say they have encountered Dogmen at Ma-Me-O Beach before. He was not surprised to hear of a possible wendigo sighting at such a location either.

Lewis heard of Knudsen's encounter. He does not doubt that the event occurred just as she remembers. He emphasized wendigo encounters cannot be investigated as a whole, as they differ from witness to witness. In some cases, there is a light, as there was in the Ma-Me-O Beach sighting. Sometimes, there is not. Other encounters are preceded by a wind-like sound, even in the absence of actual wind.

Lewis said the presence of the light in this case is particularly interesting. He encountered a witness in Minnesota who claimed to have three wendigo sightings, each accompanied by a light. In one unique encounter, the wendigo had a light on its head, almost like a star. He has often pondered this scenario.

"I wonder how much of the light got cut out of the original folklore. Maybe it wasn't noticeable, or it wasn't memorable. [When] you tell someone how to survive [an encounter], you describe the thing and not the light. Maybe it got omitted from some of the lore?"

Lewis has further postulated that if the light is a result of a portal between worlds, this could explain why a wendigo has never been captured or a corpse found.

But back to Ma-Me-O Beach – Perrault-Werner explained burial grounds are sacred places. To see a tunnel of light near one indicates something special is going on in the area. Ironically, she felt at peace and not uneasy – sensations one would not typically associate with a place where something like a wendigo might have been seen.

Knudsen agreed with this feeling. She reiterated that she felt as if pieces of what they all saw that fateful night were finally coming together. This meant, of course, that we had to go back and investigate the cemetery further!

We drove back to the site in our respective vehicles and stood on the dirt road by the cemetery. Standing there, the space seemed huge despite the limited number of crosses and memorials that were there. Most were white, although a few crosses were unpainted or painted brown. Some had flowers or balloons attached to them. I did not do a proper count but estimated about two to three dozen were scattered about the site. Oddly, there were several piles of dirt next to some of the memorials, as if the bodies were recently buried. Had they been?

I asked how safe it was to venture into the area. Perrault-Werner suggested we would be fine as long as we were respectful and entered with good intentions. I didn't have the heart to tell her I was not worried about some kind of supernatural repercussion for venturing into the cemetery. I was more concerned that we were essentially trespassing and there were homes nearby. We had no idea how people would react to us being there if we were spotted.

Taking a few steps in, it became clear that not only was the cemetery in direct line of sight to where the light tunnel had appeared, but also there was nothing in the area that could have created such an illumination. Certainly, there was nothing emitting enough light that could have penetrated the woods between here and the road. As fate would have it, had we not chosen that specific side road to drive down, we would have never known this cemetery was there.

The group spoke excitedly amongst themselves. Standing in the cemetery, everyone felt at peace, something Willow agreed she didn't feel the night of their encounter. Knudsen could not comprehend how this was all seemingly coming together.

"To think… We had no idea this was here. We'd never been in this area before and here we are. I have no words. It's not often that I'm speechless."

"It's quite special," agreed Perrault-Werner.

At that, Knudsen, Perrault-Werner, Werner, Browne, and Willow ventured off to explore the cemetery. I hung back to shoot some footage of the space. I too felt at peace here. This was not unfamiliar to me as I often feel a similar sensation in most cemeteries. It was noticeably quiet, with only the occasional bird chirp breaking through the increasing darkness.

Suddenly I heard the group's voices raise. They were in the back corner of the cemetery closest to the home. Browne held his stomach and looked ill.

"What's going on?" I asked.

"I don't feel well," Browne explained.

Perrault-Werner said she felt a heaviness in this back corner and Willow pointed out that the ground looked disturbed. She was right. It appeared as if several large holes had been dug and then filled up in this space.

The longer I stood there, the more I felt gas building up inside of me. It was as if my body wanted to burp or vomit. By that point, the group had wandered back toward the

vehicles. As I walked to rejoin them, the sensation –
thankfully – stopped.

Browne seemed visibly better as well. He had been
looking at the grave markers and noticed many were for
people who had recently died. One grave was for a thirty-
three-year-old woman who just recently passed away in
January.

Knudsen decided to grab her EMF meter from the truck
so she could try to determine why the group felt sick in the
back corner of the cemetery.

It should be noted that EMF meters are used to detect
electromagnetic fields. That is literally all that they can do.
Some paranormal researchers suggest that ghosts can
influence or manipulate these fields, thereby creating a
disturbance in the environment. The basic idea is that such a
disruption can then be visibly detected using the EMF
meter.

The problem with this, however, is that these
electromagnetic fields are everywhere and are easily
susceptible to interference. Something as simple as a
cellphone signal, a microwave going off, or even an airplane
flying overhead can cause the meter to spike. In that sense,
they are not an accurate measure for paranormal activity.

It must be stated, however, that high levels of EMF can
cause headaches, hallucinations, nausea and even anxiety –
symptoms that have long been associated with hauntings
and paranormal activity. In that sense, using an EMF meter
can be helpful in determining if an electromagnetic field is
nearby. With this information in mind, Knudsen utilized
hers to see if such a field could be responsible for the heavy
mood and ill feelings that came from this area. As she

walked toward the corner of the cemetery, Knudsen placed the meter close to the ground from time to time. Sure enough, the meter spiked a bit, indicating a level of EMF was present. She would continue to relay to the group what she was seeing.

"We're getting spikes. We shouldn't be getting anything. There's nothing electrical out here."

I pointed to some power lines in the distance, but Knudsen said they stood beyond the meter's range.

"It's not going to pick up from here and definitely not with me holding the meter down low like this."

As we walked closer to the power line, the needle on the meter should have gone up, showing an increase in EMF as we approached. Oddly, the needle didn't move. The power lines were not responsible. In fact, most of the spikes were behind us, further away from the power lines. What little spikes there were registered only a few points above zero.

One spike hit 0.4, which is within the range needed to make someone feel nausea.

"There's nothing out here," Knudsen noted of possible culprits for the sensations we had felt.

That "heady feeling" is one of the symptoms of high EMF and not uncommon in parts of Alberta. Sometimes it comes from power lines or old electrical transformers, none of which were present.

"There's a lot of places in these sorts of locations out in the middle of nowhere where we seem to be getting these rolling electromagnetic fields. It seems to be common. Don't know why. Don't know what causes it. I think we've found another spot that's doing that."

Browne was still feeling ill, so he returned to the vehicles to rest while Knudsen and the others explored the cemetery further. I spent some time filming the crosses before joining Browne, who was now watching a hockey game on his phone.

We got to talking and he expressed that there was something familiar about me. I shared that I'd noticed the same about him, so we began a line of questions to determine why. Where did you grow up? What school did you go to? The usual. None of which provided an answer.

Then Browne mentioned he'd taken a course in film acting in Vancouver. At Vancouver Film School to be exact.

"I went to Vancouver Film School!" I explained, adding I took the foundation film program and learned everything there is to know about making a movie, from writing to cinematography to editing.

That got us excited, and we quickly determined we had been at the school at the same time, 1994 to 1995. But the acting school and film program were in two different locations, so we could not have encountered each other in the halls.

However, there was one project the film and acting classes collaborated on: a training film called *Truth Is* where each film student got to direct actors in a scene. It turns out I directed Browne in one of those scenes!

Thirty years later we were back working together on another project. The world is indeed a strange place.

While we caught up on each other's lives, Knudsen returned, saying they had found what appeared to be a second, smaller cemetery just outside the fence of the main one with some odd formations in it. I joined her to take a look.

The sun was almost set as we walked there. Some of the gravesites we passed had patio lights decorating them. As they illuminated, they cast an eerie glow. When we walked into this new area, she pointed out how the grave markers were not standing in rows like the normal layout in a cemetery. Rather, they were piled together, as if they had been discarded and haphazardly tossed into piles. One of the piles was almost buried amongst a stand of small trees. A couple solitary crosses were stuck in the ground at the base of some trees.

It was like this part of the cemetery had been desecrated.

"Everywhere else these crosses are honored right? This is not," notes Knudsen.

If the mood in one part of the cemetery felt heavy, the sensation I felt here amongst these dishonored graves could best be described as creeped out. Nothing felt right back there. Perrault-Werner said it felt like we were not welcome in this space. I agreed and we decided to walk back to vehicles.

There was just enough time to update Browne on what we experienced when a large black pickup truck roared up the dirt road beside us and pulled into the cemetery, kicking up a cloud of dust and gravel as it did so. We stood in stunned silence, staring at the newcomer. The vehicle idled for a moment before the driver, who was nothing but a shadowy silhouette, turned the truck around to face us.

All of us were caught off guard, the encounter made even more alarming by the fact the truck's headlights weren't on, hence it almost appeared out of nowhere.

"We need to get out of here," Knudsen noted, speaking for all of us.

No one minced words. We all dove back into our vehicles. Werner and I started our engines simultaneously. Knudsen phoned Perrault-Werner on her cellphone.

"Just go!" was her response when asked which direction we should drive.

So, we drove back out to the main road we travelled in on before finding another route to take us to the beach, all the while keeping an eye out for that black truck. Fortunately, it didn't follow us, and we were able to find a discreet spot to park near the beach.

We were all visibly shaken by the encounter and each passing vehicle put us on edge. The vehicle and driver never resurfaced, and we agreed they were there to scare us off the burial ground. Mission accomplished.

Knudsen and the Perrault-Werner family gathered at a nearby picnic table and waited for the sun to fully set. The plan was to hang out at Ma-Me-O as late as possible in hope that a Dogman or even the wendigo would make a return appearance.

Browne remained in the truck. As the minutes neared the hour mark, it was clear he was not joining us. I walked over to see what the matter was. Did the encounter with the pickup truck spook him more than the rest of us?

"What's up, Mike? Everything OK?" I asked.

"It's my guts. They're really bad," said Browne.

Browne had been suffering from stomach woes all day. He had confided in Knudsen and I that there had been a concern for a while and it was something his doctor was looking into. I doubted the evening's excitement helped.

"Do you want to go back to Edmonton? I can drive you if you like."

Browne thought for a moment or two.

"Yeah. I think that would be best."

I let Knudsen and company know that I would be taking Browne back to the city. Knudsen and Browne are good friends, and she was quite concerned for his wellbeing. He assured her he would be alright. He explained that he just needed rest and to take some of his medication he had brought from Vancouver. We said our goodbyes for now and Browne and I drove back to Edmonton, leaving Knudsen and the Perrault-Werner waiting for whatever lurked in the dark.

Driving In Alberta

Driving in Alberta during the daytime can be a mind-numbing task: the long stretches of road with nary a curve or climb can lull you into a meditative state. Driving in Alberta at night is all the above taken to a whole new level.

For one, when it is dark, it is *dark. Really dark.* Especially on rural backroads like the ones we took to Ma-Me-O beach. There are few traffic lights. This means that for most of the return, the only illumination came from my headlights, constantly set to high beam, as well as the light from my phone, open to Google Maps so I could get back to Edmonton.

I would have fallen asleep at the wheel if Browne had not been there to keep me company. The busy day and late night following a long day of travelling left me physically and mentally wiped out. We passed the time catching up on the last thirty years, and I am convinced that kept both of us conscious. It was not winter, but the province's vast plains left me feeling very isolated. It is not difficult to imagine someone developing a psychosis if left alone out here for too long, especially during the cold months.

The trip passed in an exhausted blur, but I will never forget seeing a pair of headlights appear on the horizon. Knowing that I should turn my high beams down so as not to blind the approaching driver, I did just that. Ten long minutes later, we passed each other. This happened more than once on the drive that night. Flat, endless roads.

I dropped off Mike at his hotel and returned to mine. In an unsettling turn of events, there were several police cars outside of the building. It looked like someone was being arrested in the lobby. *You sure know how to pick places to stay, Hewlett!*

Back in my room, I texted Knudsen to let her know we were safely back and that Browne, thankfully, did not seem any worse. Unfortunately, at that time, they had yet to encounter any activity. We decided to make plans to meet at eleven later that morning, as it was well after midnight. I was beyond exhausted but too wired to sleep. It was going to be another very long day.

Despite my best intentions to sleep in, I was up by seven and hungry. So, I decided to shower and eat before reaching out to Knudsen and Browne. When we did connect, Browne advised he was feeling better and Knudsen said she and the Perrault-Werner family had an eventful night, capturing audio of what they believed were Dogmen on the prowl at Ma-Me-O beach. However, a wendigo did not make an appearance.

She played me the evening's audio when I picked her up. They recorded something canine; the sounds were almost like coyote yips but not quite. I was not there, but, if Knudsen believes she captured audio of a Dogman, then I am inclined to believe her.

Browne was waiting for us outside his hotel, bags of camera and audio equipment with him. He dove into the truck and appeared more energized than the day before. He also apologized for having to duck out early on the previous night's investigation. Knudsen and I assured him no harm was done.

"We're just glad you are doing better," she said.

Today would be a driving day. We had hundreds of miles to cover and only one day to do it. First on the agenda was to head to Slave Lake to look for the grave of Marie Courtorielle and Eating Creek. After that, we would back track through the Athabasca region to get a feel for the landscape Swift Runner inhabited. We would also stop in the Tawatinaw Valley to explore where he had murdered and eaten his family.

The drive north was uneventful, and the weather was perfect for being on the road. The smoke had cleared, and the sun was shining. Although we were all exhausted from the previous night, we did a fine job of keeping each other alert with Browne's witty sense of humor and stories about the supernatural and true crime.

Heading north, the timber became denser and greener, the stretches between forest less common. Although the landscape would never match the vast mountains of British Columbia, the terrain became less flat with the highway producing dips and valleys like gentle waves.

"It's not hard to image something like the wendigo could exist out here," Knudsen remarked. Browne and I agreed. If we ventured off the main highway, then it wouldn't take long to be in the middle of nowhere. I recalled what Lewis stated to me earlier: being in the middle of nowhere could be dangerous.

Author at Eating Creek Road Sign

Given that Eating Creek is on the outskirts of Slave Lake, we decided to make it our first stop. Much like Ma-Me-O Beach, we took a series of side roads to get there. We had no trouble finding the exact location.

I think Eating Creek must be the only wendigo encounter marked by a street sign: **Eating Creek Road**. Naturally we had to get out of the vehicle and take pictures for posterity's…and Facebook's…sake.

It was windy that day and the gusts were strong enough to cause the sign to shake in the breeze. It also ruffled the stands of largely leafless trees all around us. As for Eating Creek Road, the pavement gives way to a long unpaved roadway surrounded by trees with homesteads scattered on either side, the roofs visible above the tree line.

We got back in the truck and drove along Eating Creek Road. Knudsen eventually asked me to pull off to the left down a path cut into the tall grass by what I assume were other pickup trucks that had travelled here before us. This was less of a road and more of a trail with trees on one side and Eating Creek on the other.

The three of us got out and grabbed our equipment. Knudsen and I decided to conduct an interview with her standing off the path in the grass and trees, the creek snaking along behind her.

Knudsen noted that Eating Creek is in a district known as Lesser Slave Lake and there are people who believe the location is nothing more than a colorful name just as any other you might find in a small town. However, as Lewis already stated, it is anything but normal.

"It's actually named after a wendigo legend that existed here for decades. No one seems to know exactly when it started," she said.

She assumes it was the late eighteen hundreds when the incident occurred as that's the era when many wendigo stories in the region circulated. According to the tale, much of the townsfolk were murdered by the wendigo close to where we now stood some two hundred years later.

"Eating Creek Road still stands to this day, and, as you can see behind us, the creek is still here. The ponds are still here," Knudsen said, and turned towards the water behind her. "This is still a very, very strange legend nobody seems to be able to confirm."

The name itself is not associated with a particular person, but it is rather a reminder of what occurred at the town itself, she said.

I was, once again, struck by how vast and empty the land around us was. I pondered how these stories can thrive in such an environment. Much as I did with Ogopogo – a being I didn't think could exist until I spent time on Okanagan Lake itself – my opinions on the existence of a cannibalistic entity roaming here started to shift.

"This land is incredible," said Knudsen. "Here you can drive for days and hit absolutely nothing. No towns. Nothing."

We stood at Eating Creek in early spring. Although warm and pleasant, there was still a sense of foreboding. Knudsen asked us to imagine being here in frontier times in blowing snow and temperatures as low as minus fifty.

"There were no buildings in this part of Alberta at all, even though there are very few in this part of Alberta today. You look around and you realize how isolated and dark and cold it would have been if all you had was food and the packs on your back and you were trying to find shelter."

We stood for a while and took in our surroundings. There was just the sound of wind and rustling of dried branches for ambience. No traffic. No human voices off in the distance. Just us, the creek, and the trees. If the spirits of the two wendigo brothers remained in this area, I would not want to be around when they made an appearance.

With a few pictures taken and some footage shot, we got back in the truck, and I slowly backed out to Eating Creek Road. Knudsen plugged Slave Lake into Google Maps, and we continued our journey. Once there, we figured out the route to the cemetery, which rested atop of a hill on the outskirt of town.

The entrance to Slave Lake Cemetery is comprised of a green iron fence and large iron gate. Attached to the gate are two wreaths, one on each of the metal batwings that make up the gate itself. The trees here were a lush green and lively, a stunning contrast to what we had seen at Eating Creek a few short miles away. The rest of the cemetery is bordered by thick forest.

Behind this fence are rows upon rows of tombstones and gravesites, many adorned with fresh flowers in memory of the dead. The cemetery itself is split into two halves with a path down the middle.

We walked in and quietly made our way down the path, taking in our surroundings. Knudsen pointed out a grave belonging to the Auger family. We wondered if they were in any way related to Felix Auger, whose Indigenous name was Napanin. If you recall, he was at the center of the Trout Lake wendigo incident discussed in the early pages of this book.

"Makes you wonder," Knudsen and I said almost simultaneously.

This Auger was Martin F. Auger and lived from 1933 until 2015. Given we were hours from Trout Lake one could not dismiss a connection.

We paused at the southern edge of the cemetery and pondered where Marie Courtorielle's grave might be. As Lewis had said, the exact spot she was buried remains unknown. Knudsen's research suggested her body could be at rest on the cemetery's border. Perhaps she was buried near where we now stood?

"Her husband and her son had the difficult choice of whether or not to kill her," said Knudsen, refreshing the story in our minds. "Eventually they did. They took upon the most gruesome task and killed her with an ax."

According to legend, Courtorielle's body parts did not stop moving for about an hour after she was hacked to death. In the husband and son's mind they had mercifully put someone they loved out of her misery. The police and courts, however, did not see it that way.

"Marie normally would have been burned, traditionally, because of the wendigo," she said. "It's typically a matter of driving a stake through the body, pouring hot tallow onto the heart. All of these different traditions. And yet she wasn't burned at all."

As Lewis stated, the fact Courtorielle was not burned could mean the wendigo still lurks in the area. Although I doubted this to be the case, I have had enough bizarre encounters during my time as a paranormal investigator to not dismiss the possibility outright.

Knudsen wondered if we would be able to locate the gravesite all these decades later, so we embarked on a search of the cemetery. Having spent a lot of time in cemeteries over the years, I'm always struck by how peaceful they can be. One would assume a place that housed so many dead would feel creepy or in some way wrong, but I have never found this to be the case.

Slave Lake Cemetery was no different. Walking up and down the rows of graves and wandering the tree-lined border, I felt at ease. Even at peace. I did not, though, find any sign of some long-ago buried body. Did I really expect that we would? No, but getting here was still well worth the trip.

I regrouped with Knudsen, who had located an interesting floral display amongst the trees on the northern side of the cemetery. I suggested there were only so many places Courtorielle could have been buried, if she was even buried at the cemetery at all.

"That's just it, but I feel like if we just look around, we could probably find it," she said. "Out here, it's crazy. You could walk for a really long time and find absolutely nothing."

"That's because there's lots of nothing out here," I commented.

"There's lots of nothing and very few records. I don't think people realize how few records were kept," Knudsen lamented.

"You'd think back then they didn't feel the need to. It was a different time and when something like that happens that's so disturbing and horrible they'd just try to be done with it as quickly as possible," I suggested.

Knudsen agreed, and we made our way back to the truck while Browne snapped photos and shot video of the cemetery.

We decided to explore around the parking area and nearby woods. A cell tower stood nearby along with some sort of fenced-in structure that I could not identify. The wind had increased yet again. There was now a chill in the air despite the bright sunshine.

Looking into the woods around us, I hypothesized it would not take much for someone to disappear out here.

"If we step twenty feet in, we're gone," I noted.

"That's just it. Out here you just disappear," Knudsen added.

"Nobody gets an idea for how remote it is until you spend time up here," I said.

"This place, there sure isn't anything else like it," continued Knudsen.

Our attempts to seek out Courtorielle's grave eventually seemed futile, so we met Browne back at the truck and dug into the lunches we had packed for ourselves. As we ate, a dark-colored pickup truck rolled up, a man and a woman inside. They made no attempt to get out of the vehicle and pay respects to a fallen friend or relative within the cemetery. They just sat there.

"That's weird," said Browne, echoing what we were all thinking.

I agreed, adding this turn of events was eerily like what we had experienced last night, lest any sense of an imminent threat.

Knudsen explained that, for the most part, everyone in remote communities like Slave Lake and Eating Creek knows everyone else. Outsiders stand out and we were most definitely outsiders. She has heard of people having guns drawn on them for unknowingly wandering onto someone's property. Most folks just wanted to be left alone.

Any mention of the wendigo can draw outright hostility, she reminded us. People in these parts take these stories seriously.

The pickup's occupants eventually became bored and drove off. Were they checking out this group of strangers, hoping to scare us off for reasons we could only guess? We would never know. But it was the second time something like this had happened in just as many days. I was not willing to take any chances.

Where to go next? We toyed with the idea of travelling to Trout Lake to follow up on the Felix Auger/Napanin case, but Knudsen explained it was still a couple of hours drive north. If we decided to do that, we would then have to turn around only to drive some six hours back to Edmonton. It was already late in the afternoon. We still wanted to visit Athabasca County, which is where many wendigo stories occurred, along with the Tawatinaw Valley to explore where Swift Runner's murders took place. In the end we opted to make tracks for Athabasca County and the Tawatinaw Valley.

Athabasca County is a municipal district in north-central Alberta. The town of Athabasca, originally named Athabasca Landing, was a warehouse for the Hudson's Bay Company during the fur-trade era of the late 1800s. This warehouse facilitated the company's supply route to Lesser Slave Lake. The town eventually became the Hudson's Bay Company's headquarters for northern transport.

Much like Ma-Me-O Beach, Eating Creek, and Slave Lake, there is not much around Athabasca except for gently rolling hills and forest. The town itself is small, with a current population of less than three thousand people.

The town rests on the southern protrusion of the Athabasca River. During the fur trade, rivers were the principal means of transportation. This made the river the primary way to reach the town prior to the Canadian Pacific Railway laying tracks in the county.

Driving into Athabasca was an interesting experience. The town feels very much like a time capsule with many of the buildings appearing unchanged for decades, if not a hundred years, at least. We found evidence of this while looking at plaques in the town's park that commemorated the commercial boom of 1906 to 1914.

We parked by the railway station, which sports a vintage CP Rail car out front. We wandered around town, taking in the sights and pausing to take pictures. The red bricked Grand Union hotel, All Saints Church, and the train station itself stood out, appearing to be the oldest standing buildings in Athabasca. A particular point of interest to me was that a martial arts class was being conducted inside the train station as we walked by.

Stopping in at a local store, we became quickly aware just how noticed we were. All eyes were upon us as we walked up and down the aisles of goods. Browne purchased some Tums, as his stomach still bothered him. The older man behind the till was polite, but we were very obviously outsiders here and the people let us know it. Even Knudsen, a born-and-bred Albertan, was not from around here.

This awareness of being outsiders continued out on the streets of Athabasca. If Browne or I paused to take a picture, people stopped and stared at us. We felt scrutinized the entire time. I have travelled a lot, venturing to various countries around the world, and this is the first time I ever encountered such behavior. That is not that I felt unwelcome, but I was also cognizant that I was not being invited to stay, if that makes sense.

As I ponder this, especially looking back as I write this months later, it makes more sense that a legend like the wendigo could continue into modern times. The idea of a cannibalistic spirit that takes over people and turns them into monsters seems ludicrous by modern standards. Yet, people in these remote areas very much believe them to be true to the point that they are hesitant to even speak the spirit's name for fear of unleashing one upon them. I credit the isolationist attitude of these rural communities with that. I would not have come to that conclusion had we not literally been chased from Ma-Me-O Beach that first night, only again to come under watchful eyes at Slave Lake and Athabasca.

En route back to the truck, we decided to film a quick interview with Knudsen about Athabasca. She suggested we do it quickly and discreetly so as not to attract any more attention than we already had.

Knudsen explained the town eventually became a hub for the railways in Alberta, which contributed to increasing the county's population and making it inhabitable for Europeans.

"What's interesting is there was quite a large Roman Catholic versus Anglican battle that was going on during the late eighteen hundreds and early nineteen hundreds and they were competing for followers."

She added this is still visible today with Catholic and Anglican churches almost standing side by side in these small towns.

"All of this was very much disruptive to the First Nations communities here."

This is sadly true, as many Indigenous people were forced into the Christian faith. Their children were taken from them and placed in residential schools which essentially acted as conversion camps. Many of these schools operated into the late twentieth century.

Knudsen pointed out how unchanged towns like Athabasca are despite the passage of time.

"As soon as you step out of the car it feels like you've stepped back in time which is really an intense feeling. Many of these buildings are original. They're still here. Some are coming down, but most are from the nineteen hundreds."

As for wendigo? Athabasca County is home to wendigo stories from Trout Lake, Smokey Lake, and Slave Lake, she explained.

"This is very much the hub of the legend, for the most part, so it feels amazing to be able to walk in the shoes of some of the people who have experienced this."

Although somewhat unnerved by the reception we had received on this trip, I was getting a feel for what it would have been like to live in this far-off environment, even without the winter conditions. I was also beginning to believe how someone could be convinced a being like the wendigo haunted this landscape… and why it still could to this day.

There was one stop left on this day's adventure before returning to Edmonton: the site of the Swift Runner massacre!

As with the previous visits, the road into the Tawatinaw Valley was long and relatively straight and flat. Our route gave way to a dirt road with wide fields on either curb with forest on the far sides of each. The occasional farm or homestead was scattered about the land.

Knudsen directed me to turn onto a well-maintained side road, and I stopped just north of a small home with an old church erected next door. We got out and looked around. The valley seemed empty despite the signs of human occupants. The air was still and silent. Even the cry of birds was absent. This eerie calm was noted by Knudsen.

"It's so quiet out here now. It's hard to believe that in this area such a horrific murder actually happened. It's so quiet. It's so peaceful yet it's got such a history."

"How many people here are even aware of it?" I wondered aloud.

"That's just the thing you know. A lot of people aren't aware of the stories here because the stories aren't spoken about. They aren't discussed. Even when you talk to some of the historians, they aren't talking about some of these stories," she said.

Browne handed Knudsen a microphone to record her official on-site interview about the valley and Swift Runner. I thought it might be good to conduct this near the church, as it made for an interesting backdrop. The church looked like it had stood in that very spot for hundreds of years. I wondered if it may have brought solace to people during Swift Runner's time.

My first instinct was to approach the church via the property we passed on the way in. However, as soon as we got within sight of it, a dog started barking from inside the house, warning us off. Browne suggest asking the homeowner for permission to cross his or her property to film the interview, but Knudsen and I disagreed. We had received enough chilly receptions this day and didn't need one more, especially one involving an angry sounding dog.

I suspected those people who didn't talk about the wendigo avoided the subject not because they were unaware of Swift Runner and the other stories, but rather because they did not want to know more about them.

We agreed to conduct the interview roadside on the opposite end of the property behind a stand of trees, out of view of the dog. Every time we stepped into its line of sight it barked aggressively. We quickly figured out the best place to position ourselves where we could avoid agitating the dog.

Knudsen dug into the Swift Runner story once again, the gruesome details of which I need not repeat here. Again, we were all struck by how peaceful the valley was. I have been to murder scenes before during my time as a crime journalist. They all had an unwelcoming feel to them that was not present here. The Tawatinaw Valley felt peaceful.

However, once I put myself in the mindset of Swift Runner's last surviving boy – the last member of his family to be killed and eaten – it did not take long for that sense of dread to stir. Going back more than a hundred years, when none of the homesteads that now made up the valley existed and the land was likely made up of more dense forest, it would be easy to feel isolated and alone.

My interview with Lewis was months later, and I know now the fact he had ventured to this same vicinity in the dead of winter was beyond a risky venture. Breaking down out here, especially amongst people who genuinely did not welcome visitors would put anyone in a precarious position.

Knudsen pointed out the distance Swift Runner would have had to travel to reach Saint Albert, which was several hours away by vehicle. During his era and in the middle of winter, the journey would have taken days if not weeks. It would have most certainly been fraught with peril.

Standing here now, with the grasses and trees grown up and newer homes built, Knudsen felt the valley's horrible past had been glossed over, allowing it to become a distant, unwanted memory.

"It's an amazing, amazing place. It's interesting how history can be overgrown as the world and the landscape changes."

I asked Knudsen if she knew where exactly the Swift Runner massacre took place. Unfortunately, she did not.

"We don't know specifically where it occurred. All we have are the crime scene photos from Swift Runner's case and legal trial that the North-West Mounted Police captured upon finding his camp. But it would be somewhere pretty close to here."

Those photographs show several human bones laid out on a table in what appears to be an outside setting: the ground bare dirt. The table is covered with a blanket or cloth of some kind. The bones make up various body parts picked completely clean. There are two skulls, one much larger than the other, suggesting an adult and child.

There is also a picture of Swift Runner himself taken at Fort Saskatchewan. He was a large, beast of a man who was slightly bigger than the police officer who stood next to him. Swift Runner was clean shaven and well kept, suggesting the picture was taken shortly before his trial or even execution. His hands and feet appear to be shackled.

Looking at these photos in modern times, especially the table covered in bones, the horror of the crime quickly sets in. The previous peace I had felt disappeared. This was a place where horrible things happened, and I really did not want to be here longer than necessary.

I asked Knudsen what additional thoughts she had on Swift Runner and the Tawatinaw Valley. She thought for a moment before answering.

"These stories are an intrinsic part of Alberta. As people have come and settled here, all races and all cultures, I think this is something people do need to be aware of. This is the history of Alberta and the legal history of Alberta.

"This was the first legal hanging in the province. This is a story that is really unforgettable, and it has a lot of lessons behind it. We'll make the next leg of our journey and see where it takes us."

That leg would take place the next day. We had been on the road all day exploring and documenting. We were exhausted, and it was still a good hour to two-hour drive back to Edmonton. We needed to find our way out of the valley.

Knudsen plugged Edmonton into Google Maps, and we set off, following directions on the map. It quickly became apparent that the map's GPS was leading us deeper into the valley! Was there another route home? We were just about to switch off the map and turn around when we realized there was a turn around on the road ahead and that we would be soon travelling back the way we came. Our tired minds were just slow to clue in.

The drive home was quiet but not uncomfortable. We had completed a long day but a good one. Knudsen, Browne, and I had bonded. We were originally brought together by a mutual interest in high strangeness and the wendigo, but we had become friends out of the ensuing adventure.

Browne's mind must have been on a similar track as he spoke up.

"You know, this is what makes life worth living: adventures like this. It makes you feel alive."

Knudsen and I agreed whole heartedly. The next thing we knew we were talking about pretty much every topic under the sun, from Knudsen's pet snake to Browne's upcoming book with a little bit of local politics thrown in for good measure. I contributed as best I could while also paying attention to the unfamiliar road.

The final leg of the trip passed quickly, and the next thing I knew I had dropped off Knudsen and Browne at their respective homes before I returned to my hotel. Two days of this adventure were down. Only one remained, and if the last forty-eight hours were any indication, it would be a good one. I was tired but not like I was before this trip. I was tired because I was having a good time. I was doing something I loved with good people, and I could not wait for the experience to continue.

Browne and Knudsen at Slave Lake Cemetery

Interlude

This might be an odd confession to make in a book about a cannibalistic monster, but I've never been to Red Lobster.

Growing up in the Interior of British Columbia, there were not a lot of chain restaurants. Whenever we did travel to the coast and visit relatives in Vancouver, my family never deemed a stop at Red Lobster worthy. Despite their opinion, I love seafood, especially lobster. So, I became obsessed with Red Lobster thanks to the advertisements on television.

Years later, and much to my surprise, a Red Lobster just so happened to be located a mere five-minute drive from my hotel. Keenly aware of its proximity and very much deserving a treat after the long day on the road with Knudsen and Browne, I decided that was where I was going to eat dinner.

The drive there was easy, and I was able to find a parking spot despite the dinner hour. There was a twenty-minute wait for a table as the restaurant was full, which bode well for the meal ahead. I ordered white wine and garlic mussels as a starter and lobster and shrimp linguini as a main. The meal was well worth the several decades wait. I returned to my hotel satiated and happy.

Walking through the lobby, I noticed the pool area was empty for the first time since I had arrived. I rushed up to my room and changed into my swim trunks. For about thirty minutes, I was able to unwind with a swim in the pool's cool water and soak in the warmth of the hot tub. Then, people began to filter in, so I quickly made my way back to my room. Those thirty minutes, though, were a slice of heaven.

I had made a habit of offloading the day's audio and video each evening and did the same now. Everything was looking and sounding great! We had covered a lot of ground the last two days – both figuratively and literally – and I was happy with our progress.

Browne promised he would be emailing me a file with all his footage and recordings once he was back in Vancouver.

Pouring a whisky and dropping ice into the glass, I sat in my room's lone and well-worn cushioned chair and pondered the wendigo. Unlike my exploration of the Ogopogo, where I had gone into my research convinced such a creature could not exist, only to conclude that it did, I had yet to make such a decision with this cannibalistic folk story.

However, I was surprised by how many people I had so far encountered who did believe in the wendigo. There was a whole culture here in northern Alberta that lent itself to the existence of such a being. Not one based on the occult or paganism, but one where stories like this were allowed to remain despite the passage of time. One where old beliefs were taken seriously, despite the advancements of science and knowledge. One where outsiders were not always welcome.

The people here are not ignorant either, at least the ones I have met. They were educated people who worked hard and kept up with the times. Not to suggest that I equate belief with ignorance. I am convinced paranormal phenomena is real. I have seen it and experienced it firsthand. I have a journalism degree, a degree in film making, and an above average IQ.

At this point in my journey, it was clear to me the wendigo is a psychological phenomenon. People believed it was real. This belief allowed wendigo to manifest in people, possessing them if you will, hence Wendigo Psychosis. But Knudsen, the Perrault-Werner family, and many others believe they have seen it manifest in physical form. Such sightings have occurred for more than a hundred years, and, as we'll learn later in this book, still occur today.

I ponder if these manifestations could be a tulpa? The tulpa effect is a phenomenon where a person's mental creation becomes a semi-autonomous entity that can communicate with the person. People have reported seeing, hearing, and even touching these creations. This is not limited to the individual either, as the collective thoughts and beliefs of groups can make such being manifest.

Think this is hogwash? While theoretical in nature, the tulpa effect originates from Tibetan Buddhist mythology and mysticism where tulpas are described as etheric bodies that were created from one's unconscious/subconscious/conscious mind energy to travel to spiritual realms.

A modern example of the tulpa effect is Slender Man. Slender Man is a fictional supernatural character that originated as an Internet meme, having been created by Eric Knudsen on the *Something Awful* forum in 2009. It's since gone viral and become the subject of books, video games, YouTube videos, and a Hollywood movie.

Many people claim to have seen Slender Man in the real world and to have captured video evidence of its existence. Whether such videos are real or a hoax is a question worth asking, but there are those who are convinced the public's belief in Slender Man has essentially willed it into existence.

Belief can be a dangerous thing. Slender Man was blamed for the stabbing of a twelve-year-old girl in Waukesha, Wisconsin in May of 2014. Two twelve-year-old girls stabbed their friend nineteen times claiming they wished to commit murder as a first step in becoming proxies for the Slender Man. Both attackers were later diagnosed with mental illness and charged as adults. One of the girls claimed Slender Man watched her, could read minds, and even teleport.

This is a horrible crime but speaks to the power of belief, especially when mixed with mental illness, much like Vince Li. Could such an explanation come into play with wendigo, at least in some cases? My mind was starting to lean that way.

But what of the actual sightings of wendigo, especially ones experienced by Knudsen and the Perrault-Werner family? Could there be the manifestation of a wendigo via a tulpa, or a very real being coming into our world? I was unsure.

I was one whisky down and wanted another before bed. But first, I needed to call my son.

When away I keep in close contact with my wife and son via text message, but I always try and connect with my boy for a goodnight phone call. I had missed the previous two nights due to travel and the investigation at Ma-Me-O Beach. I was not going to pass on tonight.

Talking with Griffon is always a joy and very much indicative of his generation: that is, one that has not grown up talking on the phone. I would ask him how his day was, and he would reply with one or two words, usually "good" and "fun." School is always described as "boring," and the only time he would go into detail was when the conversation circled around to his "boring French class."

God, I missed him. And told him as such.

"I miss you too, Dad. Just two more sleeps!"

"Two more sleeps, buddy. Love you!"

"I love you, too!"

The "love you" sentiment continued in text form after we hung up, and I went to bed content not only in the knowledge that I was getting somewhere when it came to understanding the wendigo, but also that I would be reunited with my family soon enough.

The Road to Fort Saskatchewan

The third and final day of my Edmonton expedition got off to an agreed-upon late start. It would be, by far, the shortest day. Even at that, we would still cover a lot of ground, as Knudsen, Browne, and I were to be reunited with Perrault-Werner in St. Albert. This is a small community less than an hour north of Edmonton. It is also where Swift Runner appeared on a church doorstep that one fateful spring morning following the massacre of his family in the Tawatinaw Valley all those years ago. We would then set off for Fort Saskatchewan, where he was held and eventually hanged. Finally, we would stop at the former Charles Camsell Hospital where an alleged case of wendigo possession was reported.

Today was about completing our recreation of the Swift Runner story. For two full days now – and several months leading up to this trip – I had been tracking the wendigo in hope of understanding what it was. I also wanted to understand why the legend not only endured but was thriving in our modern age. I hoped today's trip would bring me even closer to that goal.

I showered, dressed, and ate breakfast with time to spare. So, I drove to West Edmonton Mall to do some exploring before meeting Browne at a section of the mall called Bourbon Street – a literal indoor street that is home to at least a dozen restaurants of every variety.

I have already described the scenery of West Edmonton Mall, so I won't bore you by repeating those details. Suffice to say, I spent a good hour wandering its floors and stores, only seeing a fraction of its expanse. However, after texting my wife several pictures of the attractions and shops, we made plans to spend our annual summer vacation here the following year.

Browne and I met up and made our way to the truck. We then picked up Knudsen and drove the thirty-minutes to St. Albert. Browne was taken with the small, quaint community that sported a mix of modern and historical architecture. I was, too finding it to be a very clean and easy-to-navigate town.

We picked up Perrault-Werner and grabbed lunch before getting down to work. Knudsen, Browne, and Perrault-Werner are all hockey fans, and that evening's game was primed to be a good one as the home team Edmonton Oilers made a bid for the Stanley Cup playoffs. Admittedly, I am not much of a National Hockey League fan and felt increasingly exhausted as the day unfolded. I quietly listened to their excited chatter while I ate, eager to get on with the day.

Our first stop was the Catholic Church where Father Lacombe encountered Swift Runner on that spring day in 1879. Perrault-Werner has a personal connection to the church, and this part of the Swift Runner story. I was eager to record it.

The short drive from the restaurant took us to a big, beautiful red-brick building adorned with a large white cross. Banners reading "Welcome" and "He Is Risen" hung from the front. Surprisingly, Knudsen led us to a small white building on the fringe of the property. As we got closer, I realized why. This was an original chapel named after Father Lacombe, and it had been lovingly preserved. We walked the outside, taking in the stark white painted boards that made up its walls. We were staring at a part of history: one that played a role in the gruesome story we were investigating.

Knudsen explained the building beside us was the oldest standing wood structure in Alberta, which is amazing in and of itself.

"But it's got a really amazing history as well. Father Lacombe was actually the man who answered the door to Swift Runner when he came knocking, claiming that he had starved throughout the winter and his family had starved to death, and he had nowhere to go."

What cast initial doubt into the minds of Father Lacombe and the other priests was that before them was a man standing six-foot-four inches and weighing more than two hundred pounds. He did not appear to have lost any weight. He was not emaciated, despite claims he had starved throughout the winter.

"Yet, he was saying his family had starved to death in this terrible winter," she said, before adding another part of Swift Runner's story that did not make sense.

"This winter hadn't been that bad. There was game. So, this is a really interesting piece of the puzzle in the Swift Runner story."

According to historical records, Swift Runner spent several nights in the company of Father Lacombe and his priests. Each night he would scream that the wendigo was coming through his window, trying to kill him

Knudsen believes this detail adds a new piece to the wendigo puzzle.

"Many people believe that wendigo cannibalism was something that happened when people were starving to death. When they didn't have any choice. And Swift Runner actually proved the rule wrong," she continued.

"So, this is a really interesting case psychologically as well. He didn't have a lack of food. He had choice. Yet he still chose to horribly murder and eat his family."

Not only is St. Albert an interesting place, but also it is an important part of the Swift Runner story and, as a result, wendigo lore.

Knudsen continued, pointing out Swift Runner walked from the Tawatinaw Valley to St. Albert, which was more than a half-hour drive on modern roads. Back in the late 1800s, before such highways and byways were built, and in the deep snow of an Alberta winter, the trek would have been a huge undertaking.

Doing the math months later, it is eighty kilometers from Tawatinaw to St. Albert (or fifty miles for my American friends).

"It would have been a slog," Knudsen said of Swift Runner's journey. "There were no roads. It was heavily forested. You've got to think about the hike it would have took and the fact Swift Runner would have camped not far from here and murdered his last child right here in St. Albert. It's pretty disturbing."

I noted that there is a town east of Edmonton named Lacombe, and asked Knudsen about this. I also wondered if the notoriety of the Lacombe name speaks to the wendigo story's prevalence in Alberta.

Knudsen nodded in acknowledgment, saying many Albertan towns are named after religious figures who came to settle in the province. However, the wendigo story does not come up in mainstream conversation that often. She said most people do not know about it.

Regardless of modern knowledge of the folklore, Priests like Father Lacombe and Father Leduc, who had towns named after them, were first-hand witnesses to alleged cases of wendigo possession.

This bit of history covered, Knudsen wanted to show us where Father Lacombe is buried, as he was laid to rest in the church's cemetery. As we made our way I felt a chill in the air despite the warm sun, which shone the brightest it had this whole trip. I shrugged it off as the persistent wind that had blown all day, but a part of my brain wondered if it was a result of walking in the path of Swift Runner and the horrible crimes he had committed.

"My parents were married in this church," Perrault-Werner said, shaking me from my thoughts.

"My grandparents were buried in this cemetery, and the service was held here, so this is a special place for us."

Perrault-Werner shared her connection with the church; one many St. Albert residents must have. However, she explained hers goes much deeper. Her great, great grandfather, Adolph Perrault, helped construct the church basement after moving to St. Albert in 1868 along with Father Lacombe.

Adolph Perrault had lived in St. Albert for eleven years when Swift Runner arrived that fateful day and lived close by when the convicted murderer knocked on the church door, she said.

"My great, great grandfather was also a volunteer for the North-West Mounted Police around the same time that the Swift Runner case happened."

"It makes you wonder; was he involved? Did he even know him?" Knudsen wondered about Adolph Perrault's involvement in the Swift Runner case.

"I get the feeling he probably did. This wasn't a huge community. It was a very small and tight-knit community, so everybody knew everybody. He was very involved with the oblates and the fathers at the mission here. I have a very strong suspicion that if he wasn't involved, he at the very least knew about what happened."

Knudsen agreed, adding Father Lacombe would have done the late 1800s equivalent of phoning 911 when he realized something was amiss with Swift Runner. As a volunteer with the North-West Mounted Police, Adolph Perrault would have been aware of what was happening.

"Swift Runner was really well known. Here's a guy who was a trapper, he was a guide, he was known in the community. I think it's fascinating and a little bit creepy that there's a connection there," she said, and looked toward Perrault-Werner.

"He may have known about all of this and even witnessed some of it."

Perrault-Werner agreed.

At that we arrived at the cemetery, which Perrault-Werner said she would guide us through, having been here several times before.

"This is a place we regularly hang out, as weird as that sounds. It's very peaceful feeling."

In addition to the deceased fathers and priests, many local Indigenous figures are buried in the cemetery. Perrault-Werner said the Catholic
Church played an import role within local Cree and Metis communities. Evidence of this lies side by side amongst the rows of gravestones and markers today.

Paved walkways crisscross the cemetery. Perrault-Werner pointed out deceased relatives and fallen figures within the Indigenous community as we made our way to Father Lacombe's grave. Many of the grave markers stood tall and were adorned with crosses. They all looked like they would be right at home in some gothic setting complete with slowly rolling fog. It felt like we had stepped into another time and place, only we were in the midst of St. Albert on a sunny spring day.

Just as with the other cemeteries we had explored during this expedition – one a day at the least – I felt completely at peace here. Even the knowledge that a murderer and cannibal had spent time on the church property did not disrupt this calm. We were literally on the trail of a being that personified evil; yet, here, amongst the dead – some of whom had direct contact with a person believed to be a wendigo – the feeling was as far removed from such horrors as it could get.

While they walked, Knudsen and Perrault-Werner discussed how this church – as was the case in most early settlements – was the center at which the community was built. The township would have been constructed around it and sprawled outward, eventually forming the modern-day cities and townships.

"You don't see it as much because of the urban sprawl," said Knudsen.

"But when you come down to these small towns like this you can really start to dig down as to where these community centers are and where their focus was at the time. You can start to peel away the layers a little bit."

Perrault-Werner led us across the cemetery, passing where her grandparents were laid to rest, stopping near a half dozen rows of small, black tombstones. This is where the church's many past fathers were buried. At the very end of one of the rows was the grave of Father Albert Lacombe, who lived from 1827 to 1916 and faced the alleged wendigo, Swift Runner.

We paused for a moment, acknowledging the historical significance of the man who not only interacted with a cannibal and murderer, but also had a town named after him. Much like visiting Eating Creek and the Tawatinaw Valley; it is one thing to read about a person of historical significance, but it is something else entirely to walk in their footsteps… or stand at the foot of their grave.

This was not Father Lacombe's original resting place. Perrault-Werner explained that he, along with a couple of other priests, was first interred in the basement of the main church: the large brick building we first encountered. He remained there until about two to three years prior to our visit when water damage to the church basement prompted the trio to be moved to the cemetery itself.

A Father Leduc, who rests behind Lacombe, also had a town named after him. Knudsen explained this is where she was born.

We wandered the cemetery for a while before making our way back to the truck. Our spirits were good, but I could tell the visit had left us feeling a bit somber, for lack of a better word. The entire expedition felt like touching a time long-ago…one tainted by the gruesome murder of a family at the hands of their patriarch.

There were two more stops to make on this journey, so I put the vehicle in drive and headed east toward Swift Runner's final resting place: Fort Saskatchewan. Unlike most of the commuting I had done in Alberta, this drive thankfully took just twenty-seven minutes. It proved to be scenic as well, as the grass and trees were starting to green. The North Saskatchewan River was visible for part of the way, adding to the natural beauty of the landscape.

Fort Saskatchewan was founded by the North-West Mounted Police. The group erected the original fort in 1875, but it no longer stands. The replica fort we visited was built in 2011 and is a major tourism draw. The region itself was a gathering place and home to many Indigenous tribes, including the Cree and Metis. It now has a population of more than twenty-seven thousand people.

As written earlier, Swift Runner was hanged at Fort Saskatchewan, the first of five such hangings at the outpost. The last one took place in 1914.

We pulled into the parking lot and got out of the truck, checking our equipment as we did so. The fort loomed large in the distance, its wooden walls standing tall above my six-foot height, the roofs of many of the buildings inside visible above them.

The gate was wide open, and we were able to walk enter without issue. In front of us stood one of the jails and a long building that looked like barracks. A common area was made up the middle of the fort where, in its original iteration, the gallows would have stood. A tower was erected at the corner of the northwest wall.

Having seen pictures of the original fort, the heritage recreation was a work of art. Everything looked exactly like the original, right down to the way the buildings were put together. Stepping through this gate felt very much like stepping back in time, a feeling that came up often during this trip.

To our left was a Murphy Wagon and Red River Cart, which rested outside of a building at the south end of the fort. Knudsen said the Red River Cart is just like the one Swift Runner was delivered in from St. Albert.

"They ended up hauling him all over this area of Alberta," she explained.

Swift Runner initially lied about what had happened to his family and where their bodies were. The Mounties spent days slogging Swift Runner around in one of these carts before he finally confessed his crimes.

"One of these carts brought Swift Runner to Fort Saskatchewan where he would eventually stand trial," she added.

The cart itself was no bigger than a small trailer and made of wooden boards and planks. A small railing ran along all four sides and stood no more than a couple feet high.

Travelling in one of these carts would not have been comfortable for the passenger or whoever was called upon to haul it, especially through deep snow.

Knudsen then led us across wooden walkways to the fort's jail, or Guard Room, as a sign above one of the doors officially labelled it. Knudsen said this building is like the one Swift Runner would have been kept in as he awaited trial. The door was locked during our visit, as Fort Saskatchewan was not open to tours at the time we were there. But Knudsen, who visited the fort before, assured us the cells inside are small and not built for comfort, as was the custom of the time.

"They're no more than a few feet wide by a few feet long with a bed in the middle of that. So, you can image what a two-hundred pound, six-foot-four/six-foot-five guy was feeling as he's trapped into one of these little cells."

The guards charged with watching Swift Runner were frightened by this large man. But it was not the acts of cannibalism that scared them; it was the fact he screamed throughout the night with terrors he was having on a regular basis. These nightmares were about a wendigo coming through his cell's window and attacking him.

"You can imagine what was going through the guards' heads as they were trying to stay overnight watching their prisoner. It was in a building, like this, where all of this took place," she said, pointing at the wooden structure behind her.

I asked Knudsen if she knew what the constables' thoughts were on the wendigo. Did they believe the stories that were clearly surfacing around them from Indigenous tribes? Or did they pass such tales off as superstition?

Knudsen said the Swift Runner case with the first time the North-West Mounted Police encountered the wendigo mythology. The act of cannibalism horrified everyone who heard the tale.

"It was in a written journal that one of the guards here expressed that he was literally too afraid of what was going on and what he was experiencing to even stay with Swift Runner. This was a brand-new thing for many of these guards. Many of them were very young and just starting out as officers, so this was a brand-new experience for them."

With no framework to compare Swift Runner's crime to, adding a supernatural element to the story – especially during a superstitious time like the late 1800s – would have been frightening. In my mind, the incident would also have allowed the wendigo mythology to spread into the settlers' mindset as well as a representation of an evil only spoken about in the Bible. It was becoming increasingly clear to me how the Swift Runner case was influencing modern belief in the wendigo, especially in Alberta.

Knudsen agreed.

"It would leave an impact."

With that in mind, we walked several paces into the common area, stopping in what appeared to be the very center of the replica fort. Knudsen said this very spot is where the gallows would have been and where Swift Runner was executed.

"He would have been marched out of his prison cell and brought out to wait for the hangman's noose."

The way Knudsen described this event, I could almost see the large cannibal being ushered out of the cell, in chains and brought to the gallows. The only difference being that the weather would have been colder and snowy in my mind, unlike the warm May afternoon we were currently experiencing.

She repeated the story I wrote about earlier: how Swift Runner became frustrated with how long it was taking for the hangman to prepare the noose for his execution.

"He was ready to go. He was bored with the fact the hangman was taking his time. This shows you the mindset of Swift Runner himself and the fact that, at this point, he wasn't concerned about being hung."

"He was ready to die," I interjected.

"He was ready to die," Knudsen repeated in agreement.

"Do you think that says something about the condition he was in and if he was aware of his mindset at this point?"

"Interestingly enough, many of the officers that had actually got to know Swift Runner said that they actually liked him as a person. This is not unusual when you look at the history of a lot of different killers. Many times, they put on a nice face for the guards and that was the case here as well," Knudsen explained.

The noose was finally placed around Swift Runner's neck, and he was hanged. However, Knudsen pointed out death did not come quickly for him. It took several minutes for his life to slip away.

"It was a rather gruesome end to a terrible murderer," she concluded.

Next up was a climb into one of the guard towers. We climbed the wooden steps to the covered platform at the top, which afforded a nice view of the surrounding area. Behind Knudsen I could see where the original fort was laid out. Two wooden structures marked the original gate Swift

Runner would have been brought through in the Red River Cart. Other wooden poles revealed the original fort's four corners.

Once he was executed, Swift Runner was not buried like most prisoners. The authorities were looking to get rid of the body as fast as possible, so he was buried – without a grave marker – somewhere on the outskirts of Fort Saskatchewan.

"The whereabouts of his burial are unknown," she said.

I wondered if some of the other means of disposing of a wendigo – melting the heart of ice with hot tallow or even burning the body – would have been performed? Knudsen pointed out this was a police jail, so no such measures would have been taken.

Being winter, the ground would have been frozen, so it is possible Swift Runner would not have been buried too deeply. Perhaps animals could have gotten to his body, leaving his remains both eaten and scattered. This would make the grave's discovery even more difficult as time wore on.

Standing in the tower once again reminded me of how vast the land in Alberta is and how desolate it would have been back in Swift Runner's time. As is, there is not much outside of the towns and cities. Back then, of course, there would have been even less habitation.

"Here now we've got seating areas and a playground and walking trails. There would have been none of that back in the time of Swift Runner and the North-West Mounted Police. This would have been very barren terrain again driving home the level of isolation and hurt that was going on in the environment of the time," Knudsen explained.

Standing there, essentially at the end of our journey into the Swift Runner story, I wondered if Knudsen had any further thoughts on the matter. She said the Swift Runner case is an important part of Alberta's history and the tale and the journey of what happened has some lessons in it.

"It really serves as a reminder that Alberta has an incredibly powerful history behind it. You can't really be in the province without feeling some of that. Even though this is a very developed province and there's lots of big cities and there's lots of businesses and what not, underneath it all we must remember that these things are there. Not everything is something physical that we can see. This whole case and this story are very much a reminder of that."

Knudsen continued, saying Swift Runner's story is a reminder to hold your families close, cherish your loved ones, and remember we are only on this planet for a short amount of time. None of us know what will happen next or when the end will come.

Her words made sense, and I pointed out our experience at Ma-Me-O Beach the other night. Communicating how finding the burial ground and encountering the driver in the black truck were unanticipated events. The outcome could have been very different. Her encounter at Ma-Me-O the previous August with Perrault-Werner and her family serves as another such example of how the unexpected and unexplained can influence our lives, often from out of nowhere.

She agreed.

"These creatures or thought forms or whatever it is or whatever your stance is on these things, these experiences happen. They are not tall tales that have existed for centuries and simply been passed down. These are legal record and documents. These things occurred.

"I think we really have to take these stories and cultures and the indigenous people who passed these stories along and we have to take them seriously."

Browne, Knudsen, and Hewlett at Fort Saskatchewan

Knudsen doesn't believe the wendigo and stories like it are simply cautionary tales to frighten children into staying in bed at night. They are an important part of the culture from which they were born.

She referenced a quote from one of her and Browne's *Supernatural Circumstances* guests:

"Folklore can be true, it can be false, but it always gets something right."

"I've found, in this work, that that is absolutely, completely, a hundred percent accurate. So, we have to listen. We have to pay attention because that's where we learn our lessons," Knudsen emphasized.

Given everything that I had experienced on this expedition, coupled with the work I have done over the years as a paranormal researcher and investigator, I could not agree with Knudsen more. These monsters that are deemed as nothing more than flights of fancy or superstition are more than that. Even if you do not believe in a wendigo or Bigfoot or Ogopogo, their place culture from which they develop is very important. That makes these small town monsters something to be respected and often something that can be teach us a few lessons. They are more than just monsters: they are an important part of the human experience on this planet.

And, sometimes, from my experience and from Knudsen's as well, they are very much real!

We made our way down from the tower and wandered about Fort Saskatchewan. Even though it is a replica, I felt very much like I had travelled back in time to Swift Runner's era. His was a very different time from ours, but the supernatural elements of the story suddenly did not seem so far-fetched. However, I wasn't quite sold on the wendigo being a flesh-and-blood creature just yet.

Although I said none of this out loud, it seemed Browne and I were on the same wavelength.

"Going to the actual location really drives things home. It's not something that we typically get to do, so I'm really grateful we got to be involved in this," Browne expressed.

"It's one thing telling the story on a podcast and it's a different thing to be putting boots-on-the-ground," Knudsen said in agreement.

Perrault-Werner, who had remained quiet during our time at Fort Saskatchewan, agreed:

"It brings a new perspective."

"It reminds us that what we're talking about is real," added Knudsen.

As a writer, researcher, and investigator, I have always preferred what Knudsen called the boots-on-the-ground approach. I do not think there is really any way you can thoroughly do this work without visiting the locations where these stories occurred. There are too many people out there – especially the skeptical ones – who are unwilling to put forth that level of effort. I often think, when it comes to skeptics especially, that it is due to a level of fear involved. A fear that they may see or learn something which will change their perspectives. Belief is a hard thing to sacrifice.

As with Knudsen and Browne, I was grateful for the opportunity to take this trip and explore with them. It brought the wendigo story to life for me in a way my previous research could not.

"That's what makes this story so compelling," Browne said, once again reading my mind.

"It's the realness of it."

With that, we walked out of Fort Saskatchewan, and, after a brief stop at the gift shop, returned to the truck. We had completed the trail Swift Runner took. There was one more stop to make before we called it a day, however. One that involved another documented case of alleged wendigo possession!

Charles Camsell Hospital and Home

Charles Camsell Hospital is considered one of the most haunted buildings in Alberta. Given its history, that should come as no surprise.

The hospital was first built as a Jesuit college in the early 1900s. It was later used as a military base for U.S. soldiers building the Alaska Highway during the Second World War. Eventually, it served as a hospital for servicemen stricken with tuberculosis and other respiratory problems.

In 1946, the federal government turned it into an "Indian sanatorium" for Indigenous people, primarily those suffering from tuberculosis, which was running rampant through First Nations populations at the time. The Canadian government organized x-ray tours which sent airplanes to remote communities across northern Canada and the prairies to screen for the disease. Anyone found with symptoms were shipped to Charles Camsell Hospital for treatment. This included men, women, children, and babies. The practice was carried out for twenty years, ranging from 1946 to 1966.

Many of those sent to Charles Camsell never made it home again.

Although the hospital's previous patients were buried twelve miles away at a former residential school in St. Albert, people claim the spirits of those who died in the hospital still reside there. No longer in operation, passersby claim to see figures in the windows. Some who have broken in to wander the darkened hallways claim weird things have happened to them. Screams have been heard coming from inside.

The hospital is also said to be the site of an exorcism related to a wendigo possession case. From the 1970s until it closed in 1996 Charles Camsell was a general acute-care facility, and the alleged possession was reported during this time.

We stopped at the hospital on the drive back to St. Albert from Fort Saskatchewan. Knudsen had been to the site before, but this was her first time back. What we encountered surprised and saddened her.

A fence encircled the Charles Camsell property, which was now a construction zone alive with the sounds of saws and heavy equipment. Condominiums were being erected on the site and the hospital itself looked like it was scheduled to be torn down in favor of the same.

Knudsen said the hospital was the source of much controversy in Edmonton, partly because it was left standing for more than twenty years after it was closed, for various reasons. The bulk of the controversy surrounds the mistreatment of Indigenous patients during its time as an Indian sanatorium.

Although the abandoned hospital that still stood on the site that May wasn't the original building, Knudsen believes the torment and trauma felt by the former patients left its mark on the grounds.

During the hospital's time as an Indian sanatorium, Knudsen's family doctor – then an intern – sat in on the exorcism of an Indigenous patient.

"Which was extremely unique and very, very rare," said Knudsen.

Her details are scarce, and I was unable to find any historical records regarding the outcome of the incident. What she could recall, though, was that the patient was a young female who believed she was possessed by a wendigo in much the same manner as the stories we have already discussed in this book. An exorcism took place, but the outcome is unknown.

Is this story true? It is difficult to believe a medical professional would invent such things. Also, given the nature of the alleged incident, it is doubtful any official documentation would occur.

Former tuberculosis hospitals are rife with similar stories. My Canadian Paranormal Society colleagues and I make an annual trip to the Gooding University Inn, a former tuberculosis hospital with a storied haunted history. So storied, in fact, that the place is now rented out to paranormal teams like ours for investigation. Although no possessions, wendigo or otherwise, occurred there, there are many similarly spectacular tales associated with Gooding. From our own experience, the building is very active.

When I began my investigative career, my first investigations were at Tranquille Sanatorium in my hometown of Kamloops. This, too, is a former tuberculosis facility that was shuttered in the 1980s and essentially left to rot. As soon as it was closed, the stories started and became local urban legend. Tales ranged from a field of dead bodies being left on the property to a deformed "pig boy" whose spirit is said to still roam the remaining buildings.

Many of these stories are untrue. That does not negate, however, that I was physically pulled into a door by an unseen presence during one of my investigations. Indeed, something paranormal is going on at Tranquille.

The point of these asides? I cannot rule out what Knudsen's doctor told her about the exorcism. However, without further details, I keep my skeptic's hat on regarding what happened.

Knudsen said the details she received from her doctor are slight, but, from the way he talked about the incident, it left a lasting imprint on him.

With that, our trip through Alberta's wendigo history came to an end.

Knudsen, Browne, and Perrault-Werner shared an excited conversation on the drive back to St. Albert. In celebration, we gathered at a local pub for a "wrap party" of sorts for the expedition's conclusion. I joined in as much as I could, but I was tired. The weight of not only this trip but also the one to Gooding not even three weeks earlier was catching up with me. Still, I had a good time working with the three of them. We had done some good, hard work. Yes, I was tired, but I was also grateful for the experience.

We said goodbye to Perrault-Werner and then drove back to Edmonton. I dropped Knudsen off first, and we hugged goodbye. We were acquaintances when this adventure began but had become good friends the last three days. Vowing to work together again one day, we waved farewell for now.

Browne and I were quiet on the drive back to his hotel, but that silence reflected nothing of our new friendship. We were simply exhausted, and, I think, we appreciated each other granting us this moment of peace. But we smiled and shook hands, he invited me to come on his *Dark Poutine* podcast, which I accepted, and said our goodbyes.

So, as quickly as our tracking of the wendigo story began, it had come to an end.

I was starving, so I pulled out of Browne's hotel's driveway, darted across four lanes of traffic, and pulled into West Edmonton Mall. Making my way to Bourbon Street, I found a ramen restaurant and enjoyed a big bowl of soup and a beer. By the time that was done, I was even more tired. I made my way back to the hotel and spent the night relaxing in my room with a couple of drinks until I could not stay awake any longer. I slept long and hard.

Breakfast was quickly consumed the next morning, my gear loaded into the truck, and I hit the road home. There was a lot of rain on the eight-and-a-half-hour drive which played havoc on my tired eyes. Fortunately, the last ninety minutes passed with bright sunshine. I don't think it ever felt so good to pull into my driveway and receive hugs and kisses from my wife and son.

The next several days was spent resting and getting my energy back. Yes, I had taken a deep dive into the Swift Runner case and the wendigo phenomena, but there was still more work to be done....and a local sighting to be investigated!

Interlude: Thoughts on the Edmonton Expedition

As with deep dive into the Ogopogo legend the previous year with by friend and colleague, Eli Watson, the trip to Edmonton in search of the wendigo was a whirlwind adventure that took days to digest.

Being there, with boots-on-the-ground in all the locations associated with the Swift Runner story, certainly drove the horrible crime home in a way that reading about it and interviewing experts on the subject matter simply could not. There were times, especially in the Tawatinaw Valley and at Fort Saskatchewan, where I could almost feel what happened – the cold, the isolation, the hopelessness, and horrible nature of the crime. It also made it far easier to understand how one could be affected by the wendigo legend itself.

The vast landscape of Alberta and the miles of rural terrain are daunting by today's standards. Several times I felt very much alone there, even with two other people in the truck. Go back in time a couple of hundred years and add feet of snow as well as subzero temperatures, and it would not take much to push anyone into the realm of desperation and madness, especially if food was scarce.

Is the wendigo a psychosis? After spending time in Northern Alberta, it is easy to believe this is the case. Everything I wrote in the previous two paragraphs coupled with the wendigo stories circulating amongst Indigenous tribes create a perfect storm of belief. If you are desperate, alone, and hungry, and are considering eating someone to stay alive, then it would be a logical leap to think a wendigo spirit is trying to possess you. People tend to latch onto the simplest solutions, especially when pressed with dire circumstances. If enough people are talking about the wendigo at the time, it makes sense to jump to such conclusions.

The superstitious nature of residents in rural Alberta, and even in urbanized centers, surprised me. Not that I am not a believer. I hunt for ghosts and monsters after all and have seen enough to convince me such things are real. But the openness people displayed about their beliefs and the wary eyes that were cast on strangers like me came as a surprise, even after Knudsen cautioned me about people's attitudes in the region.

At this point I am almost willing to say the wendigo is more in people's heads than a beast or supernatural figure wandering the forests. I say *almost willing* because there is no doubt in my mind that Knudsen and company saw what they saw on that August night. There have been sightings of similar things throughout the ages and into modern times. So, it is now time to discuss modern wendigo sightings. There is one more one more adventure that remains before I can call this investigation closed.

The Wendigo in Modern Times

Given that most of the stories you will find in books and on the Internet are of past encounters it would not be a mistake to think the wendigo is strictly a historical phenomenon. But, as alluded to earlier in this book, modern-day sightings do happen. Researchers like podcaster Kenzie Taylor believe the wendigo is a very real creature stalking through the forests of today.

The fact the wendigo has been pushed into modern pop culture thanks to comic books, movies, and an episode of the popular television series *Supernatural* means people are willing to accept that such a thing can and does exist. Investigator Chad Lewis has investigated such sightings.

These sightings can be accompanied with a sound not unlike a howling wind, he explained. This is believed to freeze the experiencer with fear, making it easier for the wendigo to catch its prey. Some encounters report the wendigo even using mimicry to trick unsuspecting people into its clutches.

"The early literature never mentions anything about mimicry or mimicking, but I've had people contact me. They have a story of being in the woods hunting, and they hear their friend talking or calling to them but later they find out the friend was miles away.

"They immediately go to [it being a] wendigo, and when I ask why, they say it's because of the *Supernatural* episode, where it was mimicking human emotion or speech," relates Lewis.

What of the light Knudsen and company saw that fateful night? This has turned up in several alleged historical wendigo encounters Lewis has come across in Minnesota. He hypothesizes that if this light is indeed a portal the creature travels through, then that would explain the lack of a carcass or bones that would signify it is a flesh-and-blood creature.

The antlers, which we have already established as more of a pop culture creation than anything else, are also responsible for some of the reports Lewis receives. People see something strange in the woods with large antlers and believe they have witnessed a wendigo. He said this is true even of people who have no idea of what a wendigo is.

He was approached by two brothers who, while at a summer camp, had separate sightings of a creature with antlers. When they got home, the brothers did their own research and came across a depiction of the wendigo.

"No doubt about it. That's exactly what we saw," they recounted to Lewis.

"But, at the time [of their sighting], they'd never heard of it," Lewis stated.

Lewis wonders if the modern wendigo has indeed evolved to have antlers or has the depiction of the creature in popular culture skewed people's perspectives? He said people have evolved over time, so perhaps the wendigo has as well.

If the wendigo is indeed out there wandering the woods, seeking human prey, Lewis is convinced it would be of supernatural nature and origin. He doubts it lives in caves year-round, although some cultures that believe in the wendigo say otherwise. They suspect that it resides underwater in lakes or other waterways.

"Like Lake Wendigo in northern Minnesota. They truly believe they found holes in the ice with huge footprints leading out of the ice, walking to the island as though the wendigo is out looking for prey."

Indigenous people believe lake monsters are water spirits residing in the lake. Some tribes claim the wendigo works in a similar way, and it lives as a spirit within the water.

Ron Murphy is unsurprised that modern wendigo sightings are on the rise, and he asserts that pop culture is responsible. Now YouTubers are not just venturing into the woods hoping to catch a Bigfoot on film to blow up their channel—they are out looking for wendigo as well!

"People are out in the woods whistling and things are whistling back, or they see some sort of humanoid figure staggering at the side of the road. So, all these things are pointing towards that wendigo type of creature," explains Murphy.

"I think it's going to be much more common for people to say they're witnessing wendigos simply because they're becoming part of our common knowledge now in the cryptid world."

I tend to agree with Murphy on this point. As the wendigo has become more prominent in popular culture, more people have come to take its existence at face value. This is something we sort of touched on in an earlier chapter.

Because people believe it's real, they begin seeing it increasingly, or they have come to believe a home or tract of land is home to – or haunted by – such an entity.

As an aside, someone who heard I was researching the wendigo suggested I investigate a rural home a couple of hours from where I live because they heard it was possessed by a wendigo. I have not yet followed up on the matter because nothing I have learned about the wendigo suggests that it possesses places, only people. I mention it now to show how a story like the wendigo can be interpreted.

Earlier in the book I teased a paranormal investigation involving a wendigo as reported by investigator Amanda Quill of *Coldspotters* in Vancouver. Given this is one of the few British Columbia encounters of which I have heard, and that it occurred during modern times, I figured it was high time we get into the nitty gritty of it.

It turns out *Coldspotters* responded to not one, but two, such sightings.

Quill said her team was called to Surrey, which is a suburb of what is known as Greater Vancouver, in 2012 after a resident reported seeing a wendigo lurking in a greenbelt known as the Green Timbers Urban Forest Park. This is one of the largest parks in the area with more than six miles of nature trails, picnic areas, a regularly stocked fishing lake and nature center. All of this within a second-growth forest. The area was completely logged by 1929 but became the province's "birthplace of reforestation," hence it is considered a second growth.

At first, Quill thought being called to a wendigo sighting was cool and exciting, given it is rare for such a thing to occur. At the time, she had not researched much about the wendigo. Once she had, however, her feelings toward the case changed due to the tragic and gruesome mythos surrounding the creature.

The first case revolved around a home near Green Timbers where several incidents of paranormal activity had been reported, said Quill.

"They had their own little haunting going on," she said.

Given the haunting, Quill is vague on the details of this sighting as the residents felt whatever they saw was related to what was going on inside their home and not some external force. However, the other sighting took place "just down the road" from the first and the couple who reported it firmly believed what they saw was indeed a wendigo.

"What they reported seeing was someone coming up to their windows at night and looking in the windows. It had big antlers, and it was very tall," said Quill.

She postulates that the couple's perspective of what they saw could have been influenced by the fact it was night, and limited lighting could have made this figure appear more monstrous. Regardless, this shape terrified them. The couple was most worried about this creature preying on the animals they kept on their property.

These two sightings became the first of many. The creature is now referred to as the Rake of Green Timbers or the Rake of Surrey.

This designation is most curious as the rake is the result of an online collaborative project in the same vein as a Creepypasta. A rake is humanoid, about six feet tall when standing, but usually moves about on all fours. It has very pale skin, a blank face, and three green eyes; one in the middle of its forehead and the other two on either side of the head. Its limbs are long and spindly and low to the ground.

What is interesting to me is the rake sounds more like a traditional wendigo than what people report seeing nowadays. The being the one couple believed they saw peering in their windows looked more like a pop culture version of the wendigo.

As the reports continued, people – Quill among them – became convinced that whatever they were seeing in the Green Timbers area was related to, or a result of, tragic events that have occurred in the Lower Mainland during the last half century.

This includes drug- and gang-related deaths. Not to mention the child murders associated with Clifford Olson, a convicted serial killer who confessed to murdering eleven children and teenagers in British Columbia in the early 1980s. Many of these murders occurred in and around the Vancouver area.

The consensus among residents is bad things can leave a mark on a place, and sometimes this energy comes back in some way, shape, or form. Quill agrees.

"I believe truly that the ground takes imprints of everything that's happening, and a lot of that energy can come back up. There are consequences to our actions, and I think that's very important, especially when you're talking about the wendigo."

It is interesting to hear this perspective used in these cases, if indeed the creature the residents of Surrey keep seeing is a wendigo. Once again, we have something unexplained being used as a cautionary tale. This mysterious creature is being credited as a wendigo largely because of how it has been portrayed in popular media. As a society, we like to place things in neat little boxes to make what is happening easier to understand. People saw something that resembled a creature called a wendigo, so they believe they saw a wendigo. It is scary and unknown and bad things have happened in the area, so this… *thing*… must be a result of that. In its own way, this conclusion makes perfect sense.

Quill said *Coldspotters* conducted several investigations at homes in the Green Timbers area between 2012 to 2014. Although they never saw the Rake of Green Timbers, they were able to tie certain paranormal activity to missing persons or deaths in the region, including the murders committed by Clifford Olson. This includes an EVP (electronic voice phenomenon) that captured the name of one of Olson's victims.

"For me, I believe that does kind of play into the wendigo spirit or rake that could be haunting the land. I think there's a lot of healing that needs to happen that is not happening."

This lack of healing includes bulldozing down the past in favor of new development and the clear cutting of forests and greenspaces to support these projects, Quill states.

Quill and I had this conversation prior to me leaving for Alberta. At about the same time I was talking with a friend of my wife's named Jason Jones. Pre-pandemic we all trained at the same martial arts school, and it quickly became clear to me that Jones, like me, was a paranormal enthusiast. He does not investigate, but he is fascinated by the subject and had consumed many books, documentaries, and podcasts. At times his broad knowledge even surpasses mine, which makes conversations with him fascinating.

On this one day, he inquired as to what was my latest project. I told him I was researching the wendigo and Swift Runner case, and his eyes went wide. He knew exactly what and who I was talking about and then dropped the bomb.

"My wife thinks she's seen a wendigo," he said.

"Do tell!"

So, Jones gave me a CliffsNotes version of what they believe happened. I will not bore you with the shortened version here as he promised to ask his wife, Carla, if she would be open to an interview. Turns out, she was! We agreed to meet after I returned from Alberta.

A bit of backstory: my hometown of Kamloops is in the Interior of British Columbia and is a major transportation hub for the province. Every highway and railway travel through it. It is a small city with a population of about one hundred thousand people, and although semi-arid in climate – meaning the environment is desert like – one only must travel a half hour to be in remote forests.

About thirty minutes east of Kamloops is the community of Pinantan Lake, which is where the Joneses live. Little more than a group of homes and one store situated around the lake which the community is named after, this village is nestled in mountainous terrain and dense woodland. For as long as I can remember, Pinantan residents have reported sightings of UFOs and Sasquatch in their area. There have also been unsubstantiated claims of Satanic activity in the community over the years.

Jones and Carla believe their home is haunted, with him sharing many strange stories of goings on inside the decades-old structure. I cannot substantiate any of this as the

Canadian Paranormal Society has yet to conduct a formal investigation.

The Kamloops region itself is home to its share of paranormal tales, including Sasquatch sightings. If you are to believe the Indigenous people, there is something in the land which contributes to this high strangeness. It is said that once you live here, it will not let you leave for any length of time. If you do happen to move away, you will eventually be brought back.

I do not know if this is true, but I have moved away a couple of times. Ultimately, I always find myself moving back despite a desire to not grow old and die in my hometown. Take of that what you will.

I agreed to meet the Joneses late one afternoon. My son was to attend a birthday party at a bowling alley and the Joneses decided they would like to bowl after work. As such, this became the location of our interview, which I recorded. The following is a transcript of that interview.

Jones started by explaining some of the activity that has gone on in their home. He explained theirs is a two-story home owned by Carla's family, with his father-in-law residing in the basement. Whenever his father-in-law wants to get their attention, he will shout up from the bottom of the stairs.

"Hey guys! I'm home" or "Hey guys! What's going on?" he will say.

One day, while Jones and Carla were in separate parts of the home away from the staircase, they heard a shout rise from the basement which sounded just like Carla's father. When they went to see what he wanted, there was no one at the bottom of the stairs!

"We search his whole place. We even went into his en suite. There was no one there," said Jones. "Basically, it was a disembodied voice."

He continued, saying they hear disembodied voices in the home from time to time. Carla said whatever is in the home has moved their bathroom mirror, which was mounted on the wall.

On this occasion, Carla had just taken a shower. At this point, the mirror was mounted where it should be. She finished, left the bathroom, and her husband went in a short time later. He stepped out immediately.

"Why did you take the mirror off the wall?" he asked.

She told him she did not remove the mirror, emphasizing that there was no way she could. It would take four or five people to safely dismount a mirror of that size.

"It's sitting on the counter," Jones told her.

"So, I went in and [the mirror] was leaning nicely against the wall and all the clips were in their places," said Carla.

Carla has lived in the house since she was nine and said the place has always seemed haunted. The family moved away for a time and another resident moved in the interim. She, too, experienced odd goings on.

"My mom has experienced stuff. My brother has experienced stuff. My dad doesn't believe," she hesitates, "Well, he does and he doesn't."

One time her father awoke in the middle of the night to the smell of cigar smoke in the room, which he could not explain. Carla said he got a phone call three hours later revealing that his best friend had died. This friend smoked cigars.

The list of paranormal activity in the house goes on and on. Jones said they have seen dark shadows in the home at night, especially when all the lights are off.

"You know when people say it looked blacker than black? Like that," he said, adding the bathroom and particularly the hallway would take on this effect.

The most terrifying experience occurred one night when Carla went to use the tiny en suite bathroom off their bedroom. Carla said she was washing her hands when she saw what she thought was the silhouette of her husband standing in the doorway.

"We have another bathroom. Go use that bathroom," she said.

The figure snorted, and Carla turned to give it her full attention. That is when she noticed it wasn't her husband. She didn't know what or who it was.

"Okay, you need to go! You don't belong here!" she told it.

It took a step towards her. She then backed up into the wall, and it lunged at her. Carla was able to duck around it and jump into bed, where Jones lay, and woke him up.

"No, no, no. This isn't happening," she remembered saying allowed.

How is all this pertinent to her wendigo sighting? As you will soon learn, there are certain similarities between these encounters and what Carla saw one night two weeks before her brother died.

Her brother struggled with addiction, which is eventually what he claimed his life. She said he had managed to get clean but was starting to slip back into old, dangerous habits once again. This put the family under a lot of stress as they tried to help him but struggled with the costs of rehab.

The encounter happened at night in January 2024 while Carla was driving back from her sister-in-law's home around eleven o'clock. At the intersection where she turns onto her street for the final leg home, there are two signs with a gap between them. Through that gap one can see Pinantan Lake.

As she rolled up to the intersection, she noticed a figure standing between the two signs, masking her view of the lake.

"It looked like a moose standing on its hind legs in a cloak," she said.

Carla couldn't believe her eyes, so she quickly looked around to see if there was any kind of light that could account for some sort of optical illusion. There was nothing. When she turned back, the figure was gone. The entire encounter lasted between five and ten seconds. When pressed, she estimated she was about three seconds away from the figure based on the speed she was driving. She wasn't sure how many feet or meters away it was.

Much like the phenomena in their house, the figure was dark. It was nothing more than a black silhouette against an already dark background, only darker. Carla said she could not see any details other than the antlers and what looked like a cloak around the body.

"Why is it so dark there? And those are antlers. Am I dreaming? I don't know!" she thought to herself.

Other than her vehicle's headlights, the only other illumination was a partial moon, neither of which seemed to contribute to what she saw.

She was home within minutes and quickly told Jones what she saw. At first, he thought she might have seen a Leshy, a forest spirit with a deer skull for a head and tree-like limbs that originated in the popular *Witcher* franchise of books, video games, and the Netflix series. Realizing this was likely a work of fiction and his wife believed she saw something that was very real, he Googled the North American equivalent of the Leshy.

"It came up with pictures of the wendigo," said Jones.

He showed Carla pictures of what he had found online, and she confirmed that was what she saw. They had never seen anything like it before or since.

What strikes Carla most is that she saw this thing and then two weeks later her brother died. Not long after that her grandmother passed away from natural causes. In fact, her brother slipped back into his addiction at about the same time she saw the figure on the road.

Given the consumptive nature of the wendigo, this is an interesting coincidence which is not lost of the Joneses either. Only in this case, Carla's brother was not driven to cannibalism, if it was indeed a wendigo she saw. Also, assuming the sighting and death are connected.

This encounter and the ones reported by Quill do share a similarity. All occur in a rural or forested area and are tied to tragedies in the community. Although not the same as the traditional wendigo stories, they are almost like a modern twist on the tale. Tunnel of light aside, Carla's report is also like what Knudsen and the Perrault-Werner family encountered.

Although it was several months after the fact, Carla's encountered presented a unique opportunity: a modern wendigo sighting close to home that could be investigated. So that is exactly what I decided to do, and I knew just who to bring along for the adventure.

Investigating the Pinantan Wendigo

Peter Renn has been investigating paranormal activity for almost thirty years, a journey that has taken him all over the world before he finally settled in Canada in the 2000s. His experiences with the supernatural started while a boy growing up in the South London town of Croydon.

Each morning at about seven o'clock, while the Renn family gathered to eat breakfast, a strange ball of light would mysteriously pass through the kitchen as they ate. These encounters happened daily and quickly became part of the family's morning ritual. They even came to name this ball of light Fred, as if it were a member of the family.

This kicked off a lifetime of paranormal research and investigation, taking Renn to locations all over the United Kingdom, Australia, the United States, and eventually Canada. I met him in 2017 when he was president of the Vancouver Paranormal Society, the oldest government registered paranormal group in North America. The team was seeking new members, and I applied, eventually becoming a lead investigator and society director, conducting investigations for the team in the Interior of British Columbia.

By 2020, Renn and his family had moved from Vancouver to my hometown of Kamloops. With the COVID-19 pandemic in full swing and travel next to impossible, Renn and I formed the Canadian Paranormal Society and focused our attention on allegedly haunted locations closer to home. In the years since we have expanded our range of investigations, even travelling into the United States for cases. We have also expanded what it is that we investigate. This has come to include both Bigfoot and UFO sightings.

Renn and I share not only a passion for the paranormal, but also a skeptical nature with a dedicated work ethic. We also have a lot of fun on our investigations, neither taking ourselves nor the work we do too seriously. Combined, he and I also tend to gather a considerable amount of data in the form of photographic, audio, and even video evidence.

When I told Renn about the alleged wendigo encounter and asked him if he wanted to join me for an investigation he replied with "wen-do-we-go?" mimicking the name of that which we were soon to be seeking.

This is how things typically play out between him and I.

We embarked on this adventure on a Friday night in late July. It was not typical wendigo weather, but I did not want to wait another five or six months for winter to arrive. It had already been a long time since the sighting, and the longer one waits, the less chance of an encounter… if there was indeed such an entity in the area to begin with.

I drove to Renn's house, and he hopped in my truck with his equipment bag in tow. Having been an investigator for as long as he has, Renn has amassed quite the collection of ghost hunting tools in his toolbox. He also builds his own equipment – everything from trigger objects to electronic spirit boards – so our team never has a shortage of tricks up our collective sleeves.

Our plan of attack, so to speak, came together on the drive up to Pinantan. We intended to use trigger objects to determine if an entity was indeed present. These are simple electronic devices that emit a light and sound when touched. When it comes to spirits, the common belief is they can manipulate the electromagnetic field that exists around us, allowing them to move objects, open doors, et cetera. Or, in the case of what paranormal investigators wish to occur, the spirits can activate a trigger object either on demand when asked or at their own will.

Failing that, we would next use a device called a Spirit Box to initiate contact with whatever lurked in the mountains around Pinantan. A controversial tool, the Spirit Box is an AM/FM receiver with a limited range. Again, the theory is that spirits and other entities can use the electromagnetic field to communicate with us via devices like the Spirit Box. The controversy stems from the fact the Spirit Box does receive radio signals in a barrage of noise that sounds somewhat like the rotors of a helicopter.

How can the listener discern what is a spirit talking versus simply the radio? We asked pointed questions that, if answer correctly, are not simple yes and no responses. These intelligent responses, as we call them, come in the breaks between AM/FM reception, the silence between the rotors turning, so to speak. Also, Renn and I were investigating on the fringe of where radio signals could be picked up. We had used a Spirit Box in the mountains outside Kamloops before and could not receive any local radio stations. We hoped this would increase our chances of success on this mission.

I asked Renn to run a GoPro for me to capture some footage on the drive up, just in case something of note happened. It did, in a way. I had driven to Pinantan many times before, and although I didn't know the area like the back of my hand, I did have directions to the spot where Carla believed she saw the wendigo. However, Renn and I could not find the location, even though it was clearly located on Google Maps and via photographs provided by Jones. It was almost like we would get close to the spot only to get turned around somehow, finding ourselves out of the community, forced to turn around, go back, and try again.

I am not implying this was paranormal, but it was certainly odd given how small the community at Pinantan is. Think a one-horse, one-stop light town, and you get the idea.

Renn decided to turn off the GoPro at one point so he could help me navigate. However, the camera refused to switch off despite several attempts to get it to do so. In the end, I had to take the battery out to shut down the device. The file was corrupted. None of the footage could be salvaged, but the camera worked fine the next time I used it. It has not given me any issues since.

Again, I am not claiming this was a paranormal occurrence either, despite having had similar malfunctions occur with video and audio equipment during paranormal investigations. There is a standing theory that spirits will drain power from electronics to manipulate the environment around them. In fact, sometimes they turn off or otherwise mess with our equipment as a result. Whether or not this is what happened here I cannot say, but it was certainly an interesting coincidence given our difficulty in finding the location where Carla had her sighting.

In the end, we pulled off the main road onto a side road and found a spot in the woods near where Carla's encounter was pinned on the map. This coincidentally happened to be where our team had conducted a Bigfoot hunt a few years back. Renn believed that if Carla did indeed see something and it was still in the vicinity, we would have a chance of finding it here. I agreed.

"Any self-respecting wendigo would hang out in the woods," I declared.

"Exactly," agreed Renn.

We parked and exited the truck. Soon we were hiking our way into the forest, which was quite dense. It was only broken up by a what looked like an old logging road that had begun to fill in with growth.

"Let's go just around the corner," Renn said, indicating a turn in the path ahead.

We hiked for a moment in silence before I had to ask:

"Do you believe in wendigos, Pete?"

Renn smiled.

"I believe in Wendy's," he said, indicating the fast-food restaurant.

We hiked a bit further and decided this spot would be as good as any. Renn set his bag on the ground. He pulled out two devices that he calls Ghost Beacons, which have ultrasonic microwave sensors in them.

"They send out microwave signals all the way around them and as soon as the signal changes, it will light up," said Renn, adding the signal has a three-meter radius.

"So, if something is there, we'll pick it up."

Although not yet dark, dusk was approaching. We hoped it would be dark enough to see the beacons when – or if – they lit up.

As Renn loaded batteries into the two devices, he noted how quiet it was. Not a single bird chirped. There was no wind, so the many branches filled with leaves and pine needles did not rustle. It was very much the cliché of being "too quiet." Did that mean we would encounter something this night?

"There aren't even crickets or grasshoppers or anything. No sound at all," I noted aloud.

Renn walked further down the path and placed one of the beacons, testing to see if it would light up enough to be visible to us. He adjusted the sensitivity a few times. Sure enough, movement within the three-meter radius prompted the beacon to glow a bright yellow.

"I can see it perfectly from here, Pete," I said.

He then set up the second Ghost Beacon far enough apart from the first to give us full coverage of the area without either of us setting them off, giving himself a pat on the back while doing so.

"I'm so smart," Renn quipped.

A Spirit Box was then pulled from Renn's bag of tricks. He fired it up, and the familiar helicopter-blade static came through immediately. Absent was the radio chatter that sometimes cut through. Renn switched off the device's antenna, further reducing the chance of outside interference.

So began our Spirit Box session in the woods. The goal was to encounter an entity that could in some way be identified as a wendigo, but truth be told, we would be happy to have an interaction with anything.

Once, in these very same woods, we communicated with a spirt that had cried out for help. The mournful voice coming through the Spirit Box almost as quickly as we turned it on. The conversation continued, the voice sounding identical the entire time, eventually identifying itself as Robert. This investigation occurred at night, so we returned later, during the day, and found a cross further down the road identifying someone had been killed in a vehicle crash. That person's name happened to be Robert Backer.

This stuff does work.

Renn began with the usual question:

"Is there anyone here who wishes to speak with us? Is there anyone here who would like to say hello?"

No response. I asked if there was anyone from the local Indigenous tribes present, but this inquiry was also met with static.

Renn and I continued, offering help to any spirit in distress. If an entity was uncomfortable talking directly to us, we suggested they communicate via the Ghost Beacons. We also asked if Robert was still present. Again, just static from the Spirit Box. The beacons remained dark.

We walked about, hoping that by moving deeper into the darkening woods we would have better luck.

I chuckled, trying to come up with a question directed at wendigos.

"What's a phrase that would even address what we came up here for?"

Renn laughed and joked:

"Are there any men here dressed as goats or deer?"

Static. Nothing but static.

"Are you hungry at all?" I asked.

Static.

"What is your name?" Renn this time.

Static for a moment... then "Hello?"

"Hello!" Renn and I replied as one.

No response.

"Did you say 'Hello'?" Renn asked.

An unintelligible word came through in the same voice.

"Can you say that louder please?" I prompted.

Static for about thirty seconds.

"Are you standing close to us?" Renn this time.

"Yes," a faint voice – the same voice – replied.

"Who are you standing closest to? I'm Jason and this is Peter."

A muffled response again in the same voice as before.

Renn held up two fingers and asked the spirit to identify the number.

"Two," it said.

"Two," we said excitedly.

"Do you know where we are?" Renn said.

"No," the voice replied.

"What country is this, mate?"

Static then something muffled.

"What year is this?" I asked.

Static.

"Are you dead?" I continued.

"Tired." Renn added, breaking the mounting tension with a much-needed joke. Humor does help in this work.

Static. Our humor was not appreciated.

Our questions continued, but whoever or whatever we had been in contact with had either lost interest or moved on. We decided to take a quick break and switch to a different model of Spirit Box.

"Hello?" The word broke through the static.

"Hello!" said Renn, pointing at me.

"This is Jason and I'm Peter. Who are you standing closer to?"

"You," the voice came back.

"You as in Peter or you as in me?"

Static.

"Can you say my name?" Renn requested.

This went on for several minutes, with responses via the Spirit Box becoming fewer and farther apart. Nor did anything want to interact with our Ghost Beacons. We did contact something that sounded like a little girl, however, when we asked if one was present, the voice told us no. This communication eventually stopped as well, even when we spaced out our questions to allow more time for a response.

The night dragged on and Renn and I grew tired. Humor became more a part of our questions, and it felt like it was time to call it.

It was then that I heard a whistle come from the woods. Renn and I turned our attention in that direction. There was nothing to see in the dim light except trees and tall grass. Nothing swayed nor moved, which would have suggested something physical had been there. There was not any breeze.

"It could have been the Spirit Box," Renn offered.

"Or a loon or something," I suggested.

168

"No," said a voice through the Spirit Box.

"Was that you whistling, then?" I asked.

No response. Just more static, which continued for a good minute before Renn asked if whatever was in the woods with us would like us to leave. The only answer was more static. So Renn asked the same question again, sterner this time.

There comes a moment in every investigation involving activity where interaction eventually subsides. Some theorize the spirits – if there are any – have spent all their energy. Others suggest the entities have lost interest or simply moved on. Perhaps there was nothing to the experience at all except group hysteria. It felt like we had reached that point in our expedition.

Believing this to be the case, I decided to ask one last question:

"Is there a spirit of a wendigo here roaming these woods?"

"Is there a man dressed as a deer… here?" Renn asked, and we both started laughing.

Something low, grumbling and unintelligible sounded from the Spirit Box.

"What'd that say?" Renn wondered aloud.

I was unsure, so I allowed a few moments to pass before asking if there were any negative spirits in the woods with us.

"No," came the response.

A negative spirit or entity is more commonly referred to in popular and religious culture as a demon, fiend, or evil spirit. It is a being that has never existed as a human being. It is an unseen force that can control or alter a person's physical, mental, or spiritual being. In a sense, this is what Indigenous people believe a wendigo to be.

Apparently, there was not one with us in the woods.

So, I asked once more if a wendigo was present.

"It's bullshit," came the response.

Renn and I stood in silence for a moment.

"Well, there's your answer," said Renn.

We asked a few more questions, none of which elicited a response. The Spirit Box was switched off and the Ghost Beacons packed away. We made our way back to the truck and drove to town, making idle small talk and jokes along the way. It had been a fun night with some interesting responses from the Spirit Box, but I could not help but feel a twinge of disappointment.

Had I really expected to have my own wendigo encounter like Knudsen and the Perrault-Werner family? No, although that would have been amazing and a nice way to cap off a book on the subject! But in the world of the paranormal – the real world, not the reel one – things like that do not often happen.

Was it that final message from the Spirit Box? The one saying the whole concept was BS? Perhaps, although the whistle we heard and grumbling, unintelligible voice which came through the Spirit Box could suggest otherwise.

Unable to come up with a satisfying reason for my discontent, I dropped off Renn and returned home. A drink and an hour in front of the television later, I went to bed. My official investigation into the wendigo had come to an end.

Final Thoughts

As a paranormal researcher and investigator who also writes books on the subjects he investigates, I have been dreading writing these final thoughts for this volume.

I began researching the wendigo phenomenon in February of 2024. The expedition to Edmonton occurred in May of that year and my own investigation into the Pinantan sighting late that summer. A good six months passed before I found myself writing this closing chapter in the book you now hold.

Does my opinion on the wendigo echo the sentiment that came through the Spirit Box that late summer night in the woods? Not at all. Too many people have seen something resembling such a creature across North America to outright dismiss the claims. More poignantly, the wendigo is an important part of Algonquin and Cree culture. It is something that is still believed in – and feared – to this day. This is also the case among Caucasian people living in areas where wendigo stories have circulated for hundreds, if not thousands, of years.

Let's not forget the historical and legal records that accompany the Swift Runner and Jack Fiddler cases.

Do I believe it is purely a kind of psychosis just as some modern-day psychiatrists would like to believe? I understand the case for it and would very much like to lean that way. However, there is anecdotally enough evidence to suggest something supernatural accompanies these cases.

I lean towards the tulpa theory I laid out in a previous chapter. At the same time, though, I do not find that explanation wholly satisfying either.

I have come to believe that is the case when it comes to wendigo. More so than any other paranormal phenomenon, it simply does not fit into a nice, neat little box. It is not purely a cryptid, but it is not just a spirit either. There are elements of possession and psychosis as well. It has been created from a culture different than our own, which makes it even more mysterious and elusive.

Whatever the wendigo is, belief in it is powerful. It is also frightening in a way which I do not associate with ghosts, lake monsters, or Sasquatch. The more I investigated it, the more questions I found. Far more questions than answers.

But that is what makes this work fun, after all, and exactly why I will continue to explore the world of the wendigo and other paranormal phenomena.

Maybe that is not the conclusion you were hoping for after reading this book, but it is the only one I can truly give with any certainty.

www.ingramcontent.com/pod-product-compliance
Lightning Source LLC
Chambersburg PA
CBHW022053020426
42335CB00012B/673